THE USBORNE BOOK OF
TREASURE HUNTING

Anna Claybourne & Caroline Young

Illustrated by Ian Jackson

Simone Boni, Luigi Galante, Nicholas Hewetson,
Joseph McEwan, Ross Watton

Designed by Lucy Parris & Laura Fearn

Edited by Judy Tatchell & Jenny Tyler

Consultant: Anne Millard

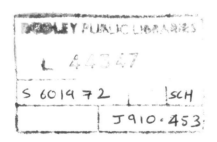
First published in 1998 by Usborne Publishing Ltd, Usborne
House, 83-85 Saffron Hill, London EC1N 8RT, England.

Printed in Spain
First published in America in 1999

CONTENTS

WHAT IS TREASURE?

When most people think of treasure, they think of gold, silver and precious stones, perhaps buried in a chest in a secret location, or lying at the bottom of the sea among the wreckage of a sunken pirate ship.

Pirate ships laden with gold are among the most popular images of treasure.

Some treasure really is like this. In the 17th and 18th centuries, thousands of ships traded gold and other valuable substances around the world. These treasure ships sometimes sank, leaving piles of gold coins and other treasure on the seabed.

Other ships were raided by pirates, who sometimes really did bury their stolen loot on remote islands, intending to collect it later. And much of this hidden treasure is still there, waiting to be found by treasure hunters.

But treasure does not have to be made of gold and silver. Anything can be treasure if people value it enough and want to find it. This can include many kinds of precious things ~ things that are very old or rare, or things that have a great historical value. Something unique and irreplaceable, like a famous painting or sculpture, or even clothes or an item of furniture can be treasure too.

WHERE IS TREASURE?

Apart from shipwrecked treasure, most treasure is buried in the ground. It was often put there on purpose. For example, the Ancient Egyptians buried huge amounts of treasure with their kings, to make sure the dead person would be rich and have everything he needed in the next life. Tombs and burial chambers filled with valuables are still being discovered today.

People also used to bury treasure to hide it, especially if it looked as if a war or invasion was about to begin. Before banks existed, the ground was the best place to keep money, jewels and silver safe from thieves. But if they were killed or imprisoned, people couldn't come back to collect their wealth, and it got left behind. Treasure like this could be buried anywhere ~ in a field near where you live perhaps.

Treasure is waiting to be discovered in all kinds of places. That's why it's so exciting. It is possible, if rare, for people to stumble upon treasure and become wealthy overnight. On the other hand, some people spend years looking and find nothing.

August Gissler, above, hunted treasure for 20 years, and only found one coin.

These ancient mummies were found in Egypt.

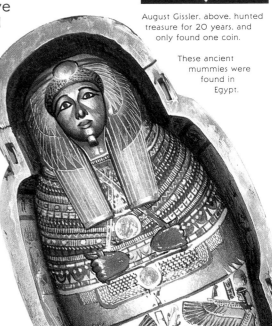

As the stories in this book show, anyone can find treasure, though some people try harder than others. Sometimes it's just luck ~ a farmworker who unearths a hoard of gold coins, or a group of soldiers stumbling on a secret tunnel.

TREASURE HUNTERS

Professional treasure hunters, however, usually know what they're looking for. They use historical information, maps and very expensive search equipment to track down a certain shipwreck or burial site. They may have to pay experts such as divers or historians, and the searches can go on for years, even decades. Many treasure hunters seek funding from rich individuals, companies or governments, to be paid back if they find treasure.

It's very important for treasure hunters to take great care of any old items they find. When Heinrich Schliemann was looking for the ancient city of Troy (see page 56), he carelessly damaged layers of old ruins. In his eagerness to find Troy, lots of precious treasure and valuable information about other civilizations was lost forever.

These days, most treasure hunters are careful and many treasure finds are cared for in museums where you can see them (see page 68).

Many treasure hunters hope to make a fortune. Some are on a more serious scientific quest, such as Robert Ballard who wanted to find the *Titanic* (see page 32). Others though, just enjoy the challenge and excitement of finding things.

FINDERS KEEPERS?

When people find treasure, they aren't automatically allowed to keep it. Often, there are laws which give a strict definition of the term "treasure". In England and Wales, all treasure which fits the definition belongs to the Crown.

Any find usually has to be reported to an official body, which then decides whether the find is treasure and who is its rightful owner.

Even in countries where finds have to be reported and offered for sale to a museum, finders are often given a financial reward, sometimes to the full value of the treasure, even if they can't keep the treasure itself.

TREASURE EXPERTS

This Ancient Greek vase showing the olive harvest tells historians something about how people used to live and work.

Archaeologists are the scientists of the treasure-hunting world. They usually look for very old treasure, especially things that reveal something about people who lived long ago.

They are often called in by other treasure hunters too, to help them and give advice. Moving or even just touching ancient things can damage them. Archaeologists know the best ways to dig objects up and then how to restore and preserve them.

This object, in the shape of a man and some musical instruments, is a jug from Ancient Greece.

5

BURIED TREASURE

Finding treasure buried in the ground is the dream of metal detector users, gold prospectors and archaeologists. There are many reasons why it might be there. Sometimes treasure hunters discover a gold or silver mine ~ after all, precious metals come from the ground to begin with.

LOST, STOLEN OR LEFT BEHIND

Large amounts of treasure have often been buried on purpose. Valuable stolen items may have been buried quickly by someone who wanted to keep his crime secret. Other people simply stored their wealth in the ground, and were carried away by disease, accidents or war before they could collect it. Precious items such as rings can also be lost by accident, especially outdoors.

These stories of treasure dug up from the earth begin in East Anglia, in the east of England. From about AD400, tribes from northern Europe, such as the Saxons, invaded eastern areas of Britain. People living there had to flee, often hastily burying hoards of treasure they couldn't carry with them. Farming methods in East Anglia mean that treasure is often found in fields.

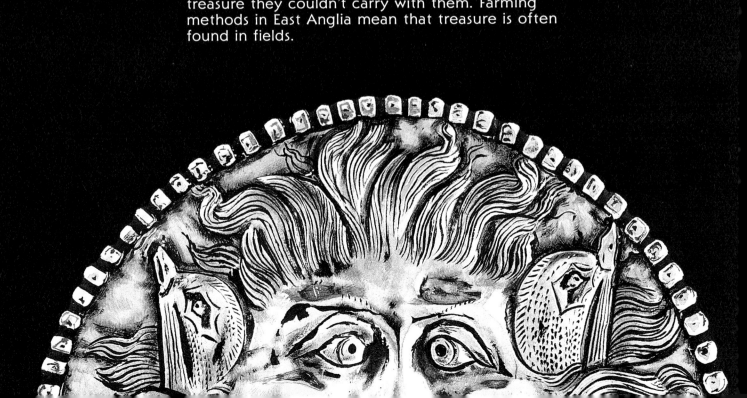

Many treasure finds involve years of searching by determined treasure hunters, but sometimes treasure is stumbled upon by accident.

CELTIC FINERY

When strange lumps of metal began turning up in a field near the English village of Snettisham, Norfolk, in 1948, the landowner decided they must be parts of an old bedstead. They were thrown into a pile in a nearby hedge.

But the pile kept growing, and at last the farmer took the objects to the local museum to see what they were. Archaeologists there were ecstatic. The "lumps" were solid gold torques, or neck rings, made by Celts who had lived in the area 2,000 years before. Over the years, more torques were found, as well as Celtic brooches, rings and coins.

Snettisham was still yielding treasure in 1990, when an amateur treasure hunter with a metal detector found a bronze vessel crammed with coins. Archaeologists rushed to the site and found more bronze and silver torques.

On the last day of the dig, ten magnificent solid gold torques were found, together with two silver torques and two precious gold bracelets.

A ROYAL TREASURY?

No one is sure why so much treasure was buried on one site. Perhaps it was a treasury, where ornaments were stored.

Many broken jewels and trinkets were found too, leading to another theory. Experts wondered whether the field was the site of a Celtic recycling depot, where old metal was melted down to make new things.

Or maybe, to hide their wealth from their enemies, tribal chiefs going into battle buried their finery in the field ~ where it remained, untouched, for over 2,000 years.

WHO WERE THE CELTS?

The Celts were a group of tribes living in northern and central Europe from about 1,000BC on. Their fierce warriors invaded Greece and Turkey, and even threatened Rome. But with the spread of the Roman Empire, from about 200BC, the Celts began to lose their power.

The Celts are famous for the artistic skill of their craftsmen, who created intricate metalwork in bronze, iron, gold and silver, often featuring distinctive swirling patterns.

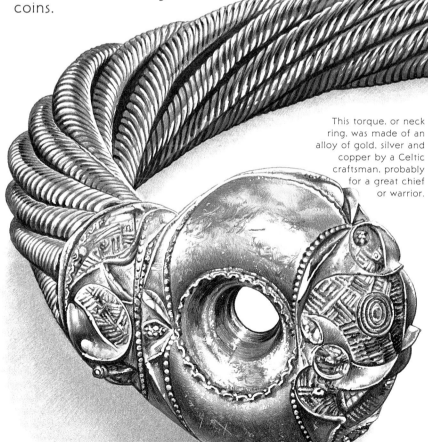

Part of a Celtic ceremonial shield, made of bronze and enamel.

This torque, or neck ring, was made of an alloy of gold, silver and copper by a Celtic craftsman, probably for a great chief or warrior.

THE HOXNE TREASURE

One day in 1992, Peter Whatling was mending a fence on his land near Hoxne in Suffolk, England when he lost his hammer. He asked a friend, Eric Lawes, if he could search for it with his metal detector.

As Lawes trod around the field, the metal detector gave a piercing squeal ~ but it wasn't caused by the missing hammer. Instead, raking through the soil, Lawes saw that he had unearthed a mass of silver coins,

The picture on the left shows an intricate gold bracelet laid out flat. Translated from Latin, the inscription on it reads: USE THIS HAPPILY, LADY JULIANA.

dulled with age. He immediately called the British Museum, who sent a team of experts to investigate.

FABULOUS FIND

Within days, archaeologist Judith Plouviez and her team began to excavate the Hoxne site. They lifted the soil in sections, so as not to disturb whatever was underneath. Then, they secretly transported the soil and its contents to the British Museum, where they began to examine what they had uncovered.

Two days later, Plouviez revealed that Eric Lawes had uncovered a 1,500-year-old Roman treasure trove ~ one of the biggest hoards of Roman treasure ever found in Britain.

As well as over 15,000 silver, gold and bronze coins, the treasure included gold chains, solid gold bracelets, silver ladles, vases, pepper pots, small silver bowls and 78 silver spoons. There were even silver toothpicks and earwax scrapers, shaped like birds and dolphins.

Archaeologists examining the hoard found numerous rusty iron nails among the valuables. From this, they guessed that the treasure must have been packed in a wooden chest which had long since decayed. This meant the collection had probably belonged to a single, very wealthy family.

RICH REWARD

The Hoxne treasure was claimed by the Crown (the British government), but Lawes didn't go unrewarded. When the British Museum bought the treasure from the Crown for its full value, a staggering £1.75 million ($2.8 million), Lawes received the same amount from the government.

He shared his fortune with Peter Whatling. When the treasure was exhibited, displayed among it was Whatling's hammer which his friend had found after all.

These beautifully carved spoons and ladles were among the 200 gold and silver tools and ornaments found in the hoard.

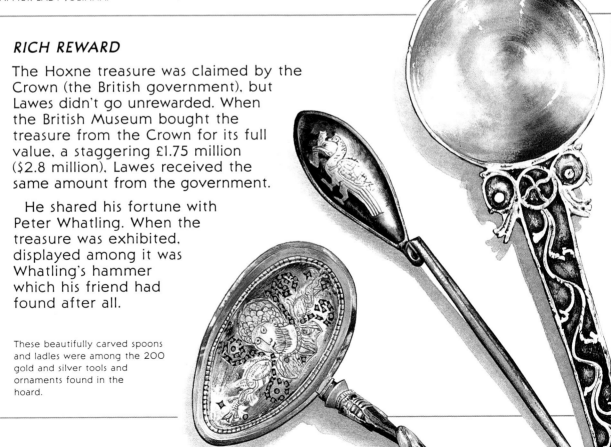

This is the central decoration on a huge silver platter, called the Mildenhall Great Dish. The dish measures 60.5cm (2ft) across.

THE MILDENHALL TREASURE

When Gordon Butcher found several dull, heavy objects all over the field he was cultivating in Mildenhall, Suffolk, in the east of England, he saw them as an obstruction to his work, and called his boss, Sidney Ford, to help him clear them away. The objects were thrown into a sack and cast aside.

It wasn't until four years later, in 1946, that Ford finally reported the find to the British Museum. As the experts cleaned off the dirt, they revealed a collection of beautifully decorated solid silver platters, goblets, ladles and bowls, made by Roman silversmiths over 1,500 years before. Many of them were engraved with the name of Lupicinus, a Roman general.

THE FAMILY SILVER

It seemed odd that the treasure had been scattered right across a field. Experts thought that the family who owned it might have had to bury it hastily while under attack from Saxons, who invaded Britain from about AD350, forcing out many of the Romans.

The hoard was worth over £6 million ($10 million), but unfortunately for Sidney Ford, he had kept the treasure for too long. He would only have been paid for it if he had reported it right away.

COCOS ISLAND

One small Pacific island became a treasure bank for a string of pirates and a magnet for treasure hunters. But even after 300 years, Cocos Island has not yet yielded up all its secrets.

Cocos Island, 500km (300 miles) off Costa Rica, Central America, has been used by at least three pirates for hiding treasure. Treasure hunters are still drawn to the island, hoping that some of its riches remain.

PIRATE BASE

In the 1680s, the English pirate Edward Davies used Cocos as a base for his ship, the *Bachelor's Delight*. He would attack passing ships and raid coastal towns before returning to the thickly wooded island to store his treasure. No one knows if he collected it all before his mysterious disappearance in 1702.

One treasure hunter's notes said an arrowhead and a carved letter "K" led to buried treasure.

This map shows possible treasure sites on Cocos Island. Although some treasure has been found, treasure hunters think more is hidden near Wafer Bay or Chatham Bay.

BONITO'S LEGACY

In 1819, a Portuguese pirate named Benito Bonito carried out a raid on the Mexican port of Acapulco, making off with a cargo of gold and silver coins. He too headed for Cocos Island, hiding his ill-gotten gains in an area known as Wafer Bay.

Two years later, Bonito was killed in a fight, leaving only a confusing map to indicate where the treasure might be.

THOMPSON'S TRICKERY

The biggest haul of all was left by a Scottish sailor, William Thompson. During a revolution in 1821, the government of Peru hired him to carry all their most valuable treasures to Panama to keep them safe. Thompson promptly stole them and buried them on Cocos Island.

The rulers of Peru forced him to take them back to the spot where he had buried the treasure, but he escaped and hid on the island until they had left. He was rescued by a whaling ship, and planned to come back to collect the treasure. But he never made it. On his deathbed, he told a friend, John Keating, where the loot could be found.

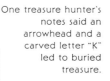

Many attempts have been made to track down the Cocos Island treasure ~ some more successful than others. In 1880, Benito Bonito's map fell into the hands of a German sailor, August Gissler, who realized that the island on the map must be Cocos. Gissler spent nearly 20 years searching on the island. All he found was one single doubloon (a Spanish gold coin), and he died in poverty.

KEATING'S ADVENTURE

In 1846, John Keating, who had been given William Thompson's treasure map, set sail for Cocos with a companion named Boag. They found the cave Thompson had described, with a hoard of treasure which included a life-size solid gold statue.

But when they returned to their ship, the crew demanded a large share of the loot and threatened violence. Keating and Boag jumped overboard and swam to the island to escape. The sailors searched in vain for the treasure, then sailed away, leaving the two men behind. Boag died, but Keating escaped on a passing whaling ship.

No one knows what he took with him, but he lived the rest of his life a wealthy man, returning to Cocos several times before his death in 1882. He left his widow clues about how to find the treasure cave, but she was never able to decode them.

These doubloons are old Spanish currency.

DEATH BY GREED

Other treasure hunters have scoured Cocos (see below), but with little success. However, in 1966, a French team found 15 gold bars and some gold coins. Nearby lay two skeletons, one with an axe clasped in one hand and a knife between its ribs, the other with a large hole in its skull. Two treasure hunters had obviously killed each other in their desperation to grab the loot for themselves.

THWARTED HOPES

August Gissler wasn't the only treasure seeker to be disappointed. In 1924, the racing driver Malcolm Campbell went to try his luck. He found nothing, but made a lot of money anyway by writing a book, *My Greatest Adventure*, about his trip.

Then, in 1932, a Belgian, Petrus Bergmans claimed that he had been a castaway on Cocos three years earlier, and that he had seen the treasure.

The photograph on the left is of August Gissler, who found one coin despite two decades spent searching.

But when he persuaded a salvage company to take him back there, he couldn't remember where it was.

In 1989 an actress named Moira Lister went to look for the treasure after inheriting a treasure map of the island. Despite spending a fortune on the search, she found nothing.

Moira Lister found that treasure hunting is not only time-consuming. The costs are huge, with no guarantee of success.

GOLD FEVER

During the American gold rush, some desperate gold-diggers would stop at nothing ~ even murder ~ to defend their hoards of treasure.

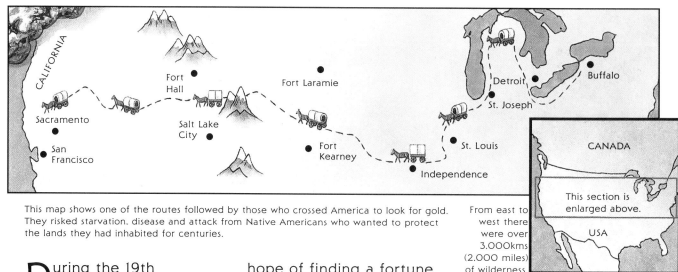

This map shows one of the routes followed by those who crossed America to look for gold. They risked starvation, disease and attack from Native Americans who wanted to protect the lands they had inhabited for centuries.

From east to west there were over 3,000kms (2,000 miles) of wilderness.

This section is enlarged above.

Duuring the 19th century, thousands of poor Europeans emigrated to America in the hope of a better life. Some were content to stay and work in the eastern states. But after gold was discovered in California on the west coast in 1848, over 80,000 people attempted the difficult and dangerous journey across the unmapped continent, in the

Very few prospectors made a fortune. Most endured back-breaking work in barren, hot desert areas.

hope of finding a fortune for themselves.

One such treasure hunter was Jacob Walz, a penniless mining engineer who came from Germany. He had tried his luck in several Californian mines without success, when news came that gold had been found in Arizona.

SACRED GOLD

Walz went to Arizona in the 1850s; but it wasn't until several years later, in 1871, that he struck lucky. One night, he rescued a stranger from a fight. The man he had saved was named Don Miguel Peralta.

Peralta told Walz that his family had struck gold on Superstition Mountain, which was the home of the Apache thunder god. The Peralta family mined

the mountain for years, exploiting its rich deposits of gold. But one day, as they were transporting a load of gold into the nearby city of Phoenix, the Apaches, angry at the destruction of their sacred land, ambushed and killed them. Only Peralta survived.

SECRET PLANS

Peralta was the only person left alive who knew where the gold mine was, and he wanted to go back to get more of its treasure. He invited Walz to join him; and they also enlisted the help of a third man, called Jacob Weiser. Peralta warned them that they would have to enter dangerous Apache territory. But Walz and Weiser were hungry for gold, and they agreed it was a risk worth taking.

Secretly, the men left Phoenix and headed for the mine. Equipped with picks and shovels, they traced the steps of the doomed Peraltas down the mineshaft. There was plenty of gold waiting to be dug out. Some versions of the story describe a glittering seam of gold 45cm (18in) thick, running through the rock.

They took turns digging and watching out for the Apaches. There was no attack, and the reward for their toil was substantial ~ gold worth $60,000 (£38,000) according to some sources. This was a fortune in 1871, and Peralta retired to live the rest of his life in comfort. But his two companions wanted more.

MURDER AND REVENGE

In 1879, Walz and Weiser decided to risk another treacherous trip to the mine. They arrived to find two Mexican men digging there. Without hesitation, they shot both men dead. The gold was not for sharing.

The local Apaches felt the same. They didn't care about the gold itself, but the land it lay in was sacred. One day, Walz left Weiser alone at the mine while he went to Phoenix. An Apache war party thundered down the mountainside, and Weiser didn't stand a chance. He was fatally wounded.

Walz settled in Phoenix, and became well-known for bragging about his gold mine whenever he was drunk. He often disappeared for a few days, to return laden with gold.

RICH AND ROTTEN

But Walz's lust for wealth had made him ruthless. He was ready to silence anyone who might spread his secret ~ and silence them for good. In 1880, two young ex-soldiers were found shot dead after boasting that they had discovered gold on Superstition Mountain. Even Julius, Walz's nephew, who had often joined his uncle on his many secret trips, was murdered.

Walz eventually died in 1891, after a final trip to the gold mine. On his deathbed, he confessed to murdering Julius. Then he used his last few breaths to spell out garbled directions to the mine:

"It lies at the spot on which the shadow of the tip of Weaver's Needle rests at four in the afternoon."

Witnesses headed for a hill called Weaver's Needle. But its shadow moved throughout the year because of the different seasons. Despite years of searching, the location of the Peralta mine has remained a mystery.

LAND FOR THE TAKING

In a cavern, in a canyon, excavating for a mine, Lived a miner, forty-niner, and his daughter Clementine.

These lines are from a song about the gold miners who flocked to the west of America in 1849. The huge migration was known as the gold rush, and those who took part in it were nicknamed forty-niners.

The government wanted new settlers, so it advertised America as a land of opportunity. Newcomers were allowed to mark out a slice of land and claim it as theirs. This angered native Americans who had inhabited America for centuries. They believed they belonged to the land rather than the land belonging to them.

Many new settlers and hopeful prospectors rallied to the government cry, "Go west!"

THE MONEY PIT

A deep and dangerous shaft, believed to contain pirate treasure, has swallowed up millions of dollars and several lives ~ and remains a compelling mystery.

On a starlit night in 1763, flickering lights were seen on uninhabited Oak Island, off the coast of Nova Scotia, Canada. News of pirate activity along the coast had intrigued those living on the mainland; and now they were convinced that Oak Island had been chosen by pirates as a place to conceal their takings.

OAK TREE TRAIL

32 years later, the tale fascinated 16-year-old Daniel McGinnis, and he rowed to Oak Island to look for the treasure. After several hours, he found an oak tree with its lowest branch sawn off. The branch above was grooved, as if a rope had been pulled across it, lifting or lowering heavy loads. Beneath the tree was a large, circular dip in the ground, as if someone had dug a pit and filled it in.

DIGGING FOR GOLD

The next day, Daniel returned with two friends, Anthony Vaughan and John Smith, to dig on the site. Their spades soon hit a layer of flagstones. They smashed through them and dug on, only to find a layer of logs. After finding two more wooden platforms, they realized someone had gone to great lengths to hide something.

Some treasure hunters have lost their lives thanks to their obsession with the Money Pit. Bob Restall, shown with his family at the top of the pit, fell into the shaft and died in 1965, along with three others.

RETURN TO THE PIT

The boys needed help to dig down further, but no one they knew had time to get involved, and they had to abandon their excavation. They finally returned nine years later, in 1804, as adults, bringing a team of men determined to get to the bottom of the pit.

Oak Island lies just off the coast of Canada, close to Chester, Nova Scotia. The island is only just over half a square km (a quarter of a square mile) in area.

Every 3m (10ft) the men dug down, they found another platform of logs. Finally, one evening, a crowbar hit something that might have been a chest. With darkness falling, they had to wait until dawn to investigate.

In the morning, to their great disappointment, seawater had completely flooded the shaft. They dug a second shaft, but that became flooded too. Daniel McGinnis eventually abandoned the hunt altogether, but he never stopped believing that treasure was hidden there.

NEW SCHEMES

In 1850, the search began again. A team from the nearby town of Truro dug a third shaft parallel to the first one, and then dug sideways. They hoped to lift out whatever had been struck by the crowbar 46 years earlier. But their excavations flooded too. Another team spent months unsuccessfully drilling in 1860, before running out of money.

The hole in Oak Island became famous, and was nicknamed The Money Pit. Over the next century, it lived up to its name, swallowing more and more money as a variety of treasure hunters tried their luck.

In 1959, Bob Restall, a former stunt rider, spent his life-savings on the

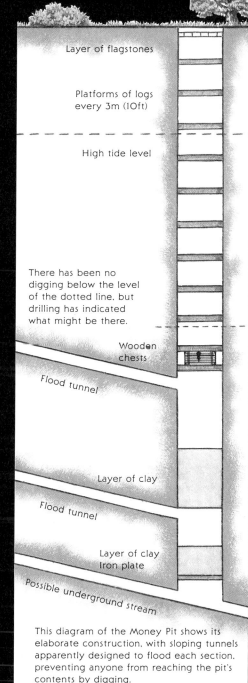

Layer of flagstones

Platforms of logs every 3m (10ft)

High tide level

There has been no digging below the level of the dotted line, but drilling has indicated what might be there.

Wooden chests

Flood tunnel

Layer of clay

Flood tunnel

Layer of clay
Iron plate

Possible underground stream

This diagram of the Money Pit shows its elaborate construction, with sloping tunnels apparently designed to flood each section, preventing anyone from reaching the pit's contents by digging.

right to dig on the island. After searching for five years, he ended up dead at the bottom of a shaft. Mysteriously, his son Bobbie and two other workers also fell in and were killed. Stories spread

that deadly fumes had seeped out and overcome them. Yet within a month, another hopeful had bought the digging rights.

HAND SHOCK

In 1969, a company called Triton Alliance began the biggest excavation so far. In the first couple of years, Triton workers found some old Mexican scissors, two pairs of shoes, and a heart-shaped stone.

Then, in 1971, Dan Blankenship, one of Triton's owners, was watching footage relayed by a camera filming inside a water-filled shaft when he saw a severed human hand float across the screen. He noticed three wooden chests nearby. But when he dived in to investigate, the walls collapsed and Blankenship was almost killed.

UNANSWERED QUESTIONS

The Triton company continued to excavate, but found nothing. Although gossip and speculation increase with each attempt on the Money Pit, it remains frustratingly unrewarding. Its complex construction suggests it was built to hide something very valuable, but some suspect that it is nothing more than a fiendishly clever hoax.

THE OXUS TREASURE

This breathtaking treasure, found in a riverbed, passed through the hands of merchants, bandits and the British army before ending up in the British Museum.

In May 1880, Captain Francis Burton, a British army officer, was in charge of a unit sent to guard a remote corner of Afghanistan, then in the British Empire. He was reading in his tent when he heard a disturbance.

Burton found his men clustered around a terrified local man who had come running into the camp for help. He said he was a servant, and that the merchants he was with had been kidnapped by bandits.

What was more, the merchants' mules had been carrying a very valuable load. Instead of their usual selection of spices and silks, they had bought gold and silver coins and ornaments from the local peasants. They were taking them to India to sell when they were attacked.

The coins and ornaments had been dug up from the dry bed of the Oxus river, where, the servant said, local people often found exotic treasures.

Captain Burton set off into the night with two men, heading for nearby caves where he thought the robbers would be. They didn't arrive until after midnight, but the sound of arguing led them to the bandits. Although the three British soldiers were outnumbered, the bandits had no guns and Burton forced them to release the merchants and hand over the treasure.

OFF TO MARKET

The grateful merchants were taken back to the camp before setting off for the Indian city of Rawalpindi (now in Pakistan). Before they left, Captain Burton himself bought one of their treasures. It was a solid gold armlet (see opposite), one of a pair.

The merchants eventually arrived in Rawalpindi, where they sold their goods. Over the next few years, two British collectors, Sir August Wollaston Franks and Sir Alexander Cunningham, collected most of it.

MUSEUM PIECES

Back home in England, Captain Burton sold his armlet to the South Kensington Museum (now the Victoria and Albert Museum). In 1897, it ended up in the British Museum, along with the rest of the Oxus treasure.

Aral Sea

Oxus (now Amu Darya) river

Oxus treasure found around here

ANCIENT BACTRIA (now Tajikistan)

AFGHANISTAN

• Kabul

• Peshawar

Rawalpindi •

Captain Francis Burton in his army uniform.

RICH HISTORY

The area around the Oxus river, now known as the Amu Darya river, has been home to various people for thousands of years. In about 400BC, it was taken over by the powerful Persian Empire, which once dominated huge areas of Asia. The Oxus treasure was probably Persian in design. The area where it was found is now covered by Afghanistan and Tajikistan.

WHERE DID THE TREASURE COME FROM?

Mystery surrounds the origins of the Oxus treasure. To this day, no one is sure where it came from, or who buried it and why. Some experts think that it might have come from a tomb or a rich temple, dating from the Persian Empire which controlled the area over 2,000 years ago. No one knows how or why it ended up in the river. It seems to have been undisturbed until the 1870s, when locals began to find it in and around the river bed, just before it came to the attention of Captain Burton.

The armlet Burton bought is made of solid gold and intricately decorated. Its purpose is not known, but it is very valuable, and also heavy and uncomfortable to wear. This suggests it would only have been worn by someone extremely rich who had no work to do, such as a king or nobleman.

This is the gold armlet that Captain Burton bought before the merchants set off for Rawalpindi. It is decorated with mythical creatures known as griffins, which are half lion, half eagle.

THE SPOILS OF WAR

Nazi treasure hidden during World War Two included not only currency, gold and valuable objects, but chilling reminders of Hitler's murderous regime.

World War Two, one of the biggest conflicts in history, began when Germany invaded Poland in 1939. The German Nazi leader Adolf Hitler hoped to create a huge empire called the Third Reich and to do this, he planned to take over most of Europe.

The Nazis did occupy several countries, but the Allied forces of Britain, America and Russia fought them back. Finally, they invaded Germany, forcing Hitler's troops into retreat. By 1945, Allied forces had bombed Berlin, the capital of Germany.

Surrounded by ruined buildings, few of Berlin's dazed survivors cared that the German national bank, the Reichsbank, had been blown apart too. But the Nazi leaders knew that Germany's last hopes in the war depended on the money and treasure the bank had been storing.

Much of this wealth did not even belong to the Nazis, but had been stolen from the countries they invaded. There were also mysterious packages sent by Hitler's ruthless military police. These packages arrived from Nazi concentration camps, such as Auschwitz, where the Nazis had imprisoned and murdered millions of people.

To keep the Reichsbank riches safe, bank officials had to smuggle them out of Berlin. On February 9, 1945, they began a three-day operation to remove thousands of sacks and crates full of money, gold and other treasure. These were loaded onto trains bound for Merkers, a small village in central Germany.

ROOM NUMBER 8

When the loot arrived in Merkers, locals and prisoners of war were ordered to unload it. They then worked for four days to lower it into the deep tunnels of the Kaiseroda potassium mine. The treasure was concealed inside a specially built vault, named Room Number 8, and secured behind a heavy steel door.

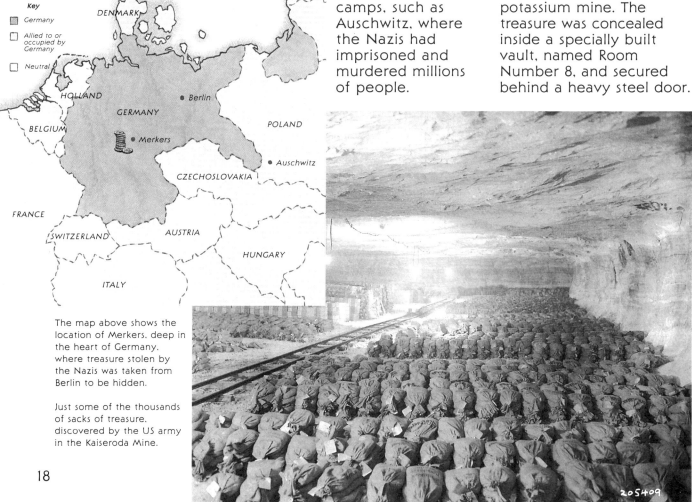

The map above shows the location of Merkers, deep in the heart of Germany, where treasure stolen by the Nazis was taken from Berlin to be hidden.

Just some of the thousands of sacks of treasure, discovered by the US army in the Kaiseroda Mine.

Key
- Germany
- Allied to or occupied by Germany
- Neutral

DENMARK
HOLLAND
BELGIUM
GERMANY
Berlin
Merkers
POLAND
Auschwitz
CZECHOSLOVAKIA
FRANCE
SWITZERLAND
AUSTRIA
HUNGARY
ITALY

205409

Just a few weeks later, however, American forces were marching through Germany, closer and closer to the treasure site. The worried Nazis decided to collect some of the loot and return it to Berlin, where cash was now desperately needed.

As bank officials hastily hauled hundreds of sacks out of the mine, their lookout raised the alarm. The Americans were coming. Panicking, the bank workers fled with 450 sacks, abandoning several hundred more in the tunnel outside Room Number 8.

GOSSIP

The Americans arrived in Merkers, where local people told them about the unusual goings-on at the mine. At first, they were ignored, but when staff from the mine confirmed the details, the officer in charge, General George Patton, decided to investigate.

On April 7, an American officer, Lieutenant Colonel Russell, descended into the mine along with mine staff, a photographer, and a museum curator named Dr. Rave, who said Reichsbank officials had ordered him to stay at the mine.

Searching the dark tunnel, the party discovered the abandoned sacks. Opening one of them, Lieutenant Colonel Russell saw that it was stuffed with banknotes.

ART TREASURES

Deeper into the tunnel, they found more money sacks, and, to their surprise, valuable and famous paintings in elegant frames, leaning against the walls. In front of them stood the steel door to Room Number 8. To look inside, they realized, they would have to blow the door open with explosives.

Precious works of art, looted by the SS (*Schutzstaffel*), the Nazi security force, were among the treasures stored in the mine.

The next morning, the group returned to the mine, taking explosives experts who blasted a hole in the wall of the Nazis' secret vault. After the dust had cleared, the investigators climbed through.

There before them, arranged in neat rows, were thousands of sacks stuffed with money, gold bars and coins. There were also suitcases filled with stolen silver and gold objects such as plates and candlesticks, flattened with hammers and ready to be melted down.

GRIM EVIDENCE

Most horrifying of all, though, were the contents of the packages and bags from Auschwitz and other concentration camps. They were

filled with tiny pieces of gold, most of them smaller than a pea. These were gold fillings taken from the teeth of thousands of Hitler's victims. Jewish people, foreigners, the disabled and many others whom Hitler considered impure and evil had been killed in the concentration camps, and their bodies raided for the tiniest traces of treasure.

The bags also contained watches, wedding rings, necklaces, bracelets and even pairs of glasses. The victims' personal possessions had been bound for the melting-pot to help fund the Nazi regime.

V.I.P. VISITOR

The discovery of the Merkers treasure soon became headline news around the world. The Supreme Allied Commander, Dwight Eisenhower, even visited the Kaiseroda Mine to look at the loot before it was taken away to be stored in Allied safes.

Without their wealth, the Nazis had no chance of regaining the upper hand. The

CROWN OF HUNGARY

One of the treasures kept in the Merkers mine was the ancient crown of Saint Stephen, a Hungarian king who died in 1031. Before the Nazis seized it, the crown had been worn by generations of Hungarian monarchs.

Instead of being sent back to Hungary, however, the dented crown was taken to Fort Knox in the USA. After the war, the relationship between the USA and communist Hungary deteriorated. The crown was only returned in 1978 after relations improved.

Allied forces were approaching Berlin, and most of the Nazi leaders fled into hiding.

Hitler himself stayed in the city, and on May 30, 1945, he committed suicide. Two days later, Berlin fell to the Allies, and on May 8 Germany finally surrendered.

Prisoners arriving at concentration camps were stripped of personal possessions such as these, which ended up as part of the Nazi treasure hoard.

A PRIEST'S HIDDEN HOARD

The villagers of Rennes-le-Château were baffled. Where on earth had their village priest come across his amazing new-found wealth?

One of the strangest of all treasure stories concerns the tiny French village of Rennes-le-Château, and its mysterious parish priest. Berenger Saunière came to the village in 1885, and was respected and well-liked when, in 1891, he was given a grant to refurbish his church.

During the restorations, the builders discovered that one of the church's columns was hollow. Inside they found four faded old parchments, which they gave to Saunière. The priest studied them carefully. Two of them contained passages from the Bible with random letters moved or inserted, like a kind of code.

Eventually Saunière went to Paris to consult some experts. When he came back, he behaved strangely. He spent the night alone in the church, and then defaced one of the tombstones in the churchyard.

Even more bizarre, Saunière suddenly seemed to be very rich. He paid for a new road, a running water supply for the village, and more expensive church renovations. For himself, he built a grand villa, a medieval-style tower and a glasshouse to display his new collection of exotic animals and birds. But he always refused to tell people how he had come by his money.

Saunière and his housekeeper, Marie Denarnaud, lived in luxury until he died in 1917 of liver failure, caused by drinking. Marie said that he had found a secret treasure supply, but she died in 1953 without revealing where it was.

A portrait of Berenger Saunière.

DECODED?

In 1970, Saunière's parchments were deciphered and two messages were revealed. The first read: *To Dagobert II, king, and to Sion belongs this treasure, and he lies here dead. Sion* means Jerusalem, and some people thought Saunière had found ancient treasure stolen from Jerusalem during the reign of Dagobert, a 7th-century French king.

The second message was stranger. It said: *Shepherdess no temptation that Poussin Teniers hold the key. Peace 681. By the cross and this horse I dispatch this demon guardian at midday blue apples.* This may be an anagram of the tombstone inscription Saunière had tried to erase. But, so far, no one has solved it.

TREASURE ISLANDS

These three islands may still contain some of the treasure hidden on them up to 300 years ago.

This is the flag of the pirate Blackbeard, a sight dreaded by sailors.

During the golden age of piracy, in the early 1700s, hundreds of pirate ships sailed the Atlantic. They were looking for Spanish treasure ships, carrying home vast amounts of wealth from Spanish colonies in South America. Some of the pirates who raided them managed to amass huge fortunes.

Most pirates probably spent their spoils quickly, and few had much left over. But some treasure really *was* buried on islands for safekeeping, just as in adventure stories and folk tales.

BLACKBEARD'S TREASURE

Blackbeard, whose real name was Edward Teach, was one of the most feared pirates on the seas. Even though his career only lasted two years, from 1716 to 1718, he was very successful. He liked to appear in a cloud of smoke, with burning fuses woven into his hair and beard. His victims were usually so scared that they handed over their cargo without a struggle.

Blackbeard's reign of terror ended after he sailed to the Isles of Shoals, a group of islands off the east coast of America. He was ambushed by a government ship, and shot dead. But when officials searched his ship, looking for his stolen treasure, they found only cocoa, sugar and cotton. Had Blackbeard buried his booty on the Isles of Shoals?

A LAST MESSAGE

One story says that the night before he died, Blackbeard left a message for anyone who hoped to find his riches. He said: "Only two people know where the treasure lies, the Devil and myself; and he who lives the longest may claim it all!" Since then, many treasure hunters have searched the Isles of Shoals; but none of the treasure has ever been found.

GALVESTON ISLAND

In 1909, two buccaneering brothers named Jean and Pierre Lafitte arrived in America from France. They set up a blacksmith's shop, but soon extended their business into smuggling, slave-trading and piracy.

In 1815, America fought the English at the Battle of New Orleans, and the Lafitte brothers left their evil ways for a while to join the war effort. As a reward, the government pardoned them and allowed them to live on Galveston Island, off the coast of New Orleans, USA, where they founded a town called Little Campeche.

Pierre disappeared, but Jean Lafitte went on to use the island as a base for piracy. He attacked numerous passing ships, and the treasure he took was probably stored somewhere on the island.

At last, the government clamped down on Lafitte and ordered him to leave Galveston Island. Furious, he burned the town of Little Campeche to the ground and sailed away in his ship, *Pride*, never to be seen again.

Treasure seekers soon flocked to the island in search of Lafitte's loot. It was said to include a buried chest full of rare jewels, marked by a wooden staff stuck into the ground.

No one managed to find the chest; but a story is told of a ploughman who decided to tie his horse to a stake while he had a snooze. When he woke up the horse had wandered off, uprooting the stake. Only then did the man realize that this might have been Lafitte's treasure marker.

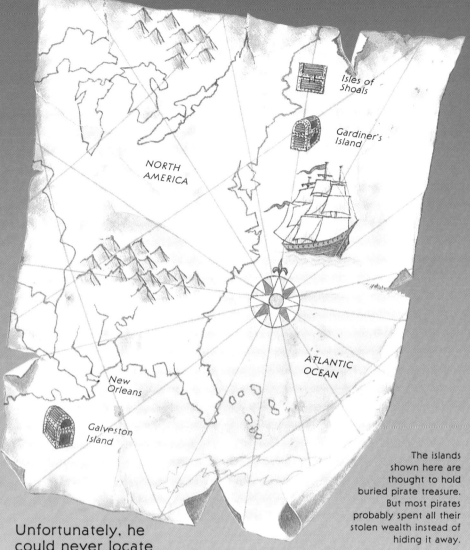

Captain Kidd's treasure was said to include gemstones and gold coins, such as these Spanish coins known as pieces of eight.

The islands shown here are thought to hold buried pirate treasure. But most pirates probably spent all their stolen wealth instead of hiding it away.

Unfortunately, he could never locate the spot again.

GARDINER'S ISLAND

On July 17, 1699, Captain William Kidd arrived at Gardiner's Island, off Long Island, USA, and was greeted by the island's owner, John Gardiner. Kidd asked politely if he could bury some of his possessions there and collect them later. Gardiner agreed and invited Kidd to stay. He was a charming guest, and even gave Gardiner's wife a parting gift of a piece of gold-embroidered fabric.

Little did the Gardiners know that Kidd was in big trouble. He had looted an Indian ship, disobeying orders from the British and American governments to attack only ships belonging to their enemy, France, or to pirates. He had needed to bury the loot to hide the evidence of his crime.

Kidd never came back to collect his spoils. In 1701 he was arrested and executed for piracy. American officials came to claim the treasure, but didn't find it all. The island may still hide a secret store of gold and jewels.

23

TREASURES AT SEA

Treasure lost at sea, usually on board a sunken ship, is probably the hardest treasure to find. First, the ship has to be located. This isn't easy, as there are no landmarks at sea. Even if it is known where a ship sank, it will rarely be on the seabed directly below. Tides and currents can move wrecks considerable distances and break them up. Wrecks are often covered in mud as well, which makes them hard to spot.

Once a wreck has been found, retrieving its cargo poses new problems. Deep-sea diving is dangerous and expensive, and it can take a long time to clear away mud, cut open the boat's structure and get to the treasure which may have been damaged itself by the years spent under water.

THE PROFESSIONALS

Because of this, treasure hunting at sea is usually a job for professionals, who only look for treasure they know exists. It also takes a great deal of money to pay for the expensive equipment needed to locate wrecks. Of course, treasure hunters only make big investments because they think their searches will pay off. Sunken treasure includes vast amounts of gold, precious stones and antiques, and can make millions for those who recover it.

GHOST GALLEONS

It took a 16-year search, involving disappointment, death and disaster, for Mel Fisher to find the elusive remains of two Spanish treasure ships.

After the discovery of the Americas, the Atlantic Ocean collected a valuable haul of shipwrecks. Spanish sailing ships called galleons made thousands of journeys between America and Europe, bringing back treasure from the many new lands Spain had colonized. Whenever a galleon sank, piles of precious metals and jewels went with it to the bottom of the sea.

A STORM STRIKES

Two such ill-fated galleons were the *Nuestra Señora de Atocha* and the *Santa Margarita*. They left Cuba for Spain on September 4, 1622, laden with gold, silver, copper and gemstones. Just a day later, both ships sank during a huge hurricane. One third of the *Margarita*'s crew and passengers were saved, but on the *Atocha*, only five people out of 265 survived, by clinging to the mast after the ship had gone down.

This diver is methodically checking the seabed, using a hand-held metal detector to look for small pieces of metal, such as clumps of coins.

Although the sunken ships were known to contain vast amounts of treasure for the taking, they stayed undisturbed for the next 350 years. No one was able to find them, despite numerous efforts, and for this reason they became known as the Ghost Galleons.

TREASURE SALVORS

In 1969, a treasure hunter named Mel Fisher set up a company, Treasure Salvors, to search for the Ghost Galleons. Fisher was once a chicken farmer, but treasure hunting had always been his hobby, and since 1962 he had worked as a prosperous treasure salvager.

His success was due to the propwash, a machine he had invented which fitted over a boat's propeller. When the propeller turned, the propwash directed a jet of water at the seabed, blasting away the mud that usually covers old shipwrecks.

During the 17th and 18th centuries, Spanish galleons like the one in this painting, laden with riches from the Spanish colonies in South America, were frequently wrecked off the Florida coast.

The map on the right shows the route taken by Spanish treasure ships on their way home to Europe.

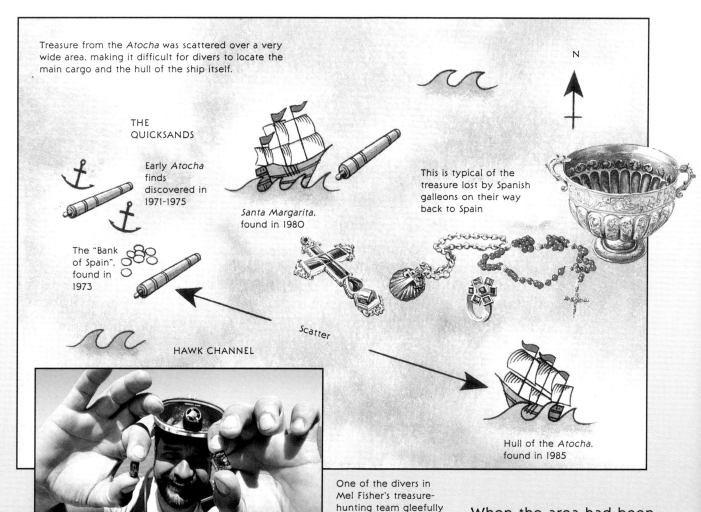

Treasure from the *Atocha* was scattered over a very wide area, making it difficult for divers to locate the main cargo and the hull of the ship itself.

N

THE QUICKSANDS

Early *Atocha* finds discovered in 1971-1975

Santa Margarita, found in 1980

This is typical of the treasure lost by Spanish galleons on their way back to Spain

The "Bank of Spain", found in 1973

Scatter

HAWK CHANNEL

Hull of the *Atocha*, found in 1985

One of the divers in Mel Fisher's treasure-hunting team gleefully holds up for the camera newly discovered emeralds, found on the ocean floor.

Fisher had made so much money out of previous wrecks that he could afford to set up his own company. His boat, *Holly's Folly*, began the search in 1969 in an area called the Middle Keys, near Florida, where Spanish records stated the *Atocha* had sunk.

But Fisher found nothing, so he hired an expert in 17th-century Spanish history, named Eugene Lyon, to help. Lyon realized what had gone wrong. Some of the islands in the area had

been renamed and *Holly's Folly* was looking in the wrong place. Lyon now redirected the search to the tiny Marquesas Keys, and Fisher was sure that they would find the *Atocha* within days.

BALL AND CHAIN

It took two more years, however, before the first sign of a shipwreck came to light. On June 12, 1971, the search ship's magnetometer (a kind of marine metal detector), indicated something on the seabed.

When the area had been cleared by the propwash, a huge anchor was revealed. Wrapped around it was a solid gold chain, and nearby Fisher found a Spanish musket ball. When the diving team found gold bars, guns and silver coins, they were sure the wreck was near ~ but there was no sign of it. The search continued in vain for the next two years.

TREASURE TRAIL

The next find, in 1973, was even more tantalizing: an area of seabed littered with over 4,000 silver coins. Among them were three silver ingots, stamped with numbers which proved they came from the *Atocha*.

The find was so valuable that Fisher named the area the "Bank of Spain". But although they followed the "scatter" ~ the trail of coins and other debris ~ the ship itself was nowhere to be found.

TRAGEDY AT SEA

There was another two-year wait before the next find. Fisher's son Dirk located some rusty cannons, which had belonged to the *Atocha*, on the seabed. But just a few days later, Dirk, his wife and another diver were drowned when their boat capsized and sank during the night.

Fisher was devastated. He was bereaved and in debt, and there was still no sign of the *Atocha*. It began to seem like a ghost ship after all.

PLAN B

But rather than giving up, Fisher decided to change his plans. Instead of a fruitless search for the *Atocha*, his team would concentrate on finding the *Margarita*.

After studying survivors' accounts, they discovered wreckage scattered in an area called the Quicksands.

Treasure such as the gems shown here, carried from South American colonies by Spanish ships, made Spain the richest country in 17th-century Europe.

They followed the trail, finding silver coins, an anchor, a cauldron, and eventually a trail of silver and gold ingots. Then, at last, they found pieces of wood, half-buried in the sand. They were gazing upon what was left of the *Margarita*'s hull.

TWO YEARS OF TREASURE

The stream of treasure from the *Margarita* kept the divers busy for two years. One of the strangest finds was a clump of silver coins, fused into the shape of the rotted wooden chest that had held them. Later, 43 solid gold chains were found and journalists named the *Margarita* the "Gold Chain Wreck".

The treasure made more than £25 million ($40 million) at auction, giving Fisher wealth as well as fame. But he could not rest until he had found the *Atocha* and early in 1985, he resumed the search.

He followed a trail of scatter into an area of deep water called the Hawk Channel. The magnetometer showed that something was there; and in April he struck lucky, finding gold bars, silver coins and uncut emeralds. More finds followed. Fisher knew he had retrieved some of the treasure from the *Atocha*, but not all of it.

July 16, 1985, saw the biggest haul so far. Silver coins, gold chains and bars, and copper ingots were piled onto the deck. Fisher knew the *Atocha* had been carrying hundreds of silver ingots and chests of silver coins ~ and four days later, these were found at last on the ocean floor, close to the *Atocha*'s hull. It had taken 16 years, but at last Fisher had found both the wrecks he had set out to find.

THE *VASA* COMES HOME

Sunken ships often appeal to treasure hunters because of the precious objects that might be on board. But in some cases, the ship itself is the treasure.

The warship *Vasa* was intended to be the pride of the Swedish navy, a testimony to the power and wealth of the great Swedish king, Gustav II. It took a thousand oak trees and over three years to build, and when it set off on its maiden voyage on August 10, 1628, the dockside was crowded with cheering citizens.

DISASTER

But disaster struck as soon as the *Vasa* left the dockside. The crew fired a cannon salute, the sails filled with a gust of wind, and almost immediately the *Vasa* tilted and fell over. Water poured in through the open gunports, and the boat sank in minutes. Over 50 people were drowned, and the ship itself was lost in the muddy waters of the Baltic Sea.

The *Vasa* setting off from Stockholm on its doomed maiden voyage.

MUD AND MURK

For over 300 years, the *Vasa* lay on the seabed, until in 1953 a Swedish engineer called Anders Franzen decided to look for it.

Franzen tried diving in the sea channels near Stockholm, but the murky water meant he could hardly see, and he was in danger of being hit by ships in Stockholm's busy shipping lanes. He tried trawling the waters with grappling hooks. He pulled up some old bicycles and other rubbish, but no evidence of the sunken warship.

LETTER CLUE

Franzen decided to do some research before continuing his quest. Eventually he found a letter to King Gustav, dated August 1628, which described the sinking. It said that the *Vasa* had gone down in 37m (120ft) of water, near an island called Beckholmen.

BACK TO THE OCEAN

Franzen was now able to locate the wreck site using a core sampler, a machine that collected cork-sized chunks from the seabed. In 1956, the sampler produced pieces of blackened oak wood, spread over a ship-sized area on the seabed.

Many personal items, such as this purse belonging to a sailor, went down with the *Vasa*.

Franzen needed to investigate what he had found, and he persuaded a local diving school to help him. One of the diving instructors, Per Edvin Falting, was the first to dive. At first, Falting saw nothing. Then, just as he was about to return to the surface, he felt the side of the ship, and found two gunports which told him that this must be the *Vasa*.

SAVE THE *VASA*

News that the wreck had been found spread fast, and a national campaign was launched to raise the ship. A salvage company offered to help free of charge, and King Gustav Adolf VI ordered the divers of Sweden's navy to offer their help too.

FRANZEN'S PLAN

Although many ingenious methods were suggested, Franzen settled on a traditional "hammock" of cables, suspended between two large ships,

to lift the wreck to the surface.

Teams of divers spent two years clearing away mud and digging tunnels under the wreck to thread the cables through. Some divers almost died when tunnels collapsed on them; but at last the cables were in place, and the *Vasa* was carefully moved into shallower waters.

ADDED STRENGTH

But the ship couldn't yet be brought out into open air because it would have collapsed under its own weight. To strengthen it, workers replaced bolts, refitted planks and made the hull watertight again. Then, four huge rubber rafts were placed under the wreck to cushion it as it rose to the surface.

Water was pumped out of the hull, and at last the *Vasa* floated again. It was towed back to the dock to the sound of cheering,

The *Vasa* was designed to be a splendid and inspiring sight as well as a deadly battleship. The oak beams and supports were decorated with intricate carvings.

just as on its maiden voyage.

Scientists and archaeologists restored the *Vasa* to its former glory, and the ship has become a national treasure and tourist attraction.

WHY DID SHE SINK?

When the *Vasa* was built, the Swedish didn't know much about large warships, and they hired a Dutch shipbuilder to design one for them. Gustav II wanted his ship to look as impressive as possible, so the designer gave it lots of high decks, packed with showy rows of guns. Unluckily, this made the *Vasa* very top-heavy, and too unstable for the open sea.

The *Vasa* in a dry dock, after being rescued from the sea and before being restored and refitted.

The *Mary Rose* was a normal warship when it was first built. To make it the pride of the fleet, it had been expanded and refitted to carry 60 guns. Holes were cut in the sides of the hull to make gunports just above the water level, which was a new technique in the mid-16th century; but these gunports probably contributed to the swift sinking, because they let all the water in as the ship began to lean to one side.

THE *MARY ROSE*

An undignified end for a spectacular ship

In 1545, France was planning a naval attack on England. A fleet of English warships was ready for battle and waiting in Portsmouth. King Henry VIII was having dinner on board one of the ships when the invading French force was spotted, and as his ships turned to face the enemy, he headed for the safety of dry land.

UNDER THE WAVES

As he watched, however, he was horrified to see the *Mary Rose*, the most lavish ship in his fleet, tilt dangerously to one side and begin to sink. Within minutes it was underwater, and 650 of the 700 men on board were drowned.

When the French saw the *Mary Rose* sink, they thought they'd scored a direct hit, but the disaster was probably caused by problems with the ship's design. New guns added during a refitting may have made it too heavy, and there were also too many men on board ~ 700 instead of the ship's usual capacity of 415.

RAISE THE ROSE

Four hundred years went by before anyone came up with a plan to salvage the *Mary Rose*. A journalist, Alexander McKee, and an archaeologist, Margaret Rule, formed the Mary Rose Committee in 1967. Their aim was "to find, excavate, raise and examine" the famous ship's remains.

Henry VIII, above, displayed his wealth and status by building grand warships. He was especially proud of the *Mary Rose*, described as "the flower of all ships that ever sailed."

The text below, taken from a painting of the *Mary Rose*, may be part of an inventory.

RAISING THE HULL

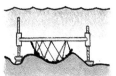  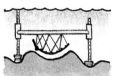 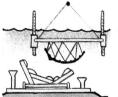 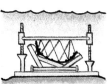 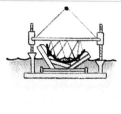

1. To lift the *Mary Rose*'s hull, a steel frame was lowered over it and attached with strong wire cables.

2. A steel cradle, lined with cushioning airbags, was then lowered into the water next to the hull.

3. The steel frame was jacked up, gradually lifting the hull clear of the seabed.

4. A crane lifted the steel frame carrying the hull into position over the cushioned cradle.

5. The hull was then lowered gently down to rest on the cradle, which was specially shaped to hold it.

6. The crane lifted the whole structure out of the water and placed it on a barge to be towed home.

It wasn't hard to find the wreck. Working in secret to avoid a media frenzy, McKee and Rule scanned the seabed and located a long, ship-shaped object in the exact place where, 132 years earlier, divers had claimed to have spotted the *Mary Rose*.

As with the *Vasa* (see page 28), mud had to be cleared from around the vessel. Divers found a 16th-century gun, then timbers from the ship's hull, which they spent years measuring and recording.

By now, the search was no longer a secret. McKee and Rule formed the Mary Rose Trust, with Prince Charles as president, and gathered support and funding from all over the world.

At last, in 1979, the salvage operation began. Everything inside the hull ~ from weapons and everyday objects, to the ship's inner structure ~ was brought piece by piece to the surface, where it could be reassembled later.

The hull itself had been eaten into by shipworms and damaged by the tides, so it could not float on its own. Instead it was raised onto a barge to be floated home to Portsmouth (see above).

REBUILDING

The timbers had spent so long underwater that they were in danger of falling apart. The *Mary Rose* and everything on board had to be rebuilt and restored under carefully controlled conditions, and preserved with chemicals.

The hull of the *Mary Rose* being rebuilt in an atmosphere of tightly controlled humidity.

AN ICY GRAVE

The Titanic *was not only the most famous wreck in maritime history ~ it was also one of the deepest. How could it ever be found?*

The *Titanic* became the most famous shipwreck of all time when, in the early hours of April 15, 1912, it sank to the icy depths of the North Atlantic after hitting an iceberg. There were over 2,200 people on board, and around 1,500 of them died in the disaster.

The massive passenger liner was designed to be the height of luxury, and had been declared practically unsinkable. The ship's maiden voyage was a major event, and those on board included several American millionaires.

There were also 915 crew to serve, entertain and cook for the excited passengers.

When disaster struck, however, it became clear that the ship's owners, the White Star Line, had not thought of everything. Although other ships in the area had radioed iceberg warnings, the *Titanic's* radio officer was off duty. The ship's construction, made up of 16 compartments, was supposed to be able to survive any collision ~ but the iceberg ripped through five of them and water flooded the ship.

Worst of all, the *Titanic* only had enough lifeboats for 1,180 people. In the confusion, many of them set sail only half full.

The *Titanic*, accompanied by tugboats, undergoing a sea trial near Belfast, where it was built, before heading for Southampton where it set out on its famously ill-fated maiden voyage.

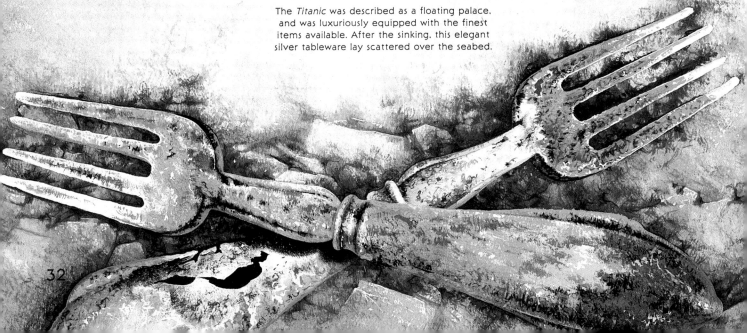

The *Titanic* was described as a floating palace, and was luxuriously equipped with the finest items available. After the sinking, this elegant silver tableware lay scattered over the seabed.

Finding the *Titanic* became a dream for treasure hunters. The wealthy passengers were reported to have been carrying priceless jewels and diamonds, although some experts say these stories aren't all true. However, because of the *Titanic*'s legendary status, even everyday items on the wreck now have great value for collectors.

AQUATIC AMBITIONS

In 1973, a young oceanographer named Robert Ballard decided he wanted to find the lost liner. He didn't want to make money ~ he was more interested in achieving the scientific feat of locating such an inaccessible wreck. No one had ever retrieved anything from a ship as deep as the *Titanic*. She lay in over 4,000m (13,000ft) of freezing cold water off Cape Race, Newfoundland, Canada.

Ballard's employers, the Woods Hole Oceanographic Institute, agreed with his plans and lent him a ship called the *Alcoa Seaprobe*.

MAKING PREPARATIONS

Ballard borrowed several pieces of expensive equipment, including a sonar scanner which could locate solid objects underwater by bouncing sound signals off them. He had a magnetometer too, to detect metal objects, and a camera for taking pictures of the seabed. These tools were all placed in a secure capsule, or "pod", which could be lowered beneath the ship.

Now Ballard needed to work out exactly where to look, and Bill Tantum, a member of the Titanic Historical Society, offered to help. Using evidence from the *Titanic*'s SOS messages, along with information about winds and sea currents,

they calculated the best place to begin the search.

The *Alcoa Seaprobe* finally set out in October 1977, its first mission to test Ballard's impressive array of equipment. But after only a few days, it all went horribly wrong. Ballard and his crew were woken in the night by a loud crash.

POD PERIL

A vital piece of piping had snapped, causing a heavy weight to crash onto the deck. The weight had been counterbalancing the pod which dangled below the ship ~ and the pod and all the borrowed equipment inside it had sunk to the bottom of the sea.

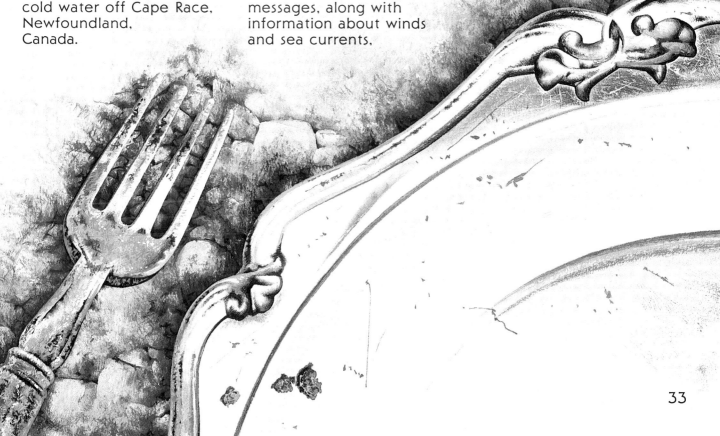

THE RACE IS ON

Unsurprisingly, Robert Ballard's employers were not impressed. They withdrew the loan of the oceanographic vessel and he was left with no means of continuing his search.

Meanwhile, a Texan oil tycoon named Jack Grimm announced that he too planned to find the *Titanic*. He poured huge amounts of money into his search, but after three expeditions he had found nothing. This only served to renew Ballard's ambitions. He wanted to get there first.

NEW BACKERS

This time Ballard asked the US navy to help him build a computer-controlled mini-submarine, called a submersible. This would be pulled beneath a ship and use sonar and video to record everything it "saw". It would then transmit live pictures to a video monitor on board the ship.

By 1985, two submersibles were ready. One was called ANGUS (Acoustically Navigated Geological Underwater Survey). The other, the *Argo*, was named after an adventure ship in Greek legend.

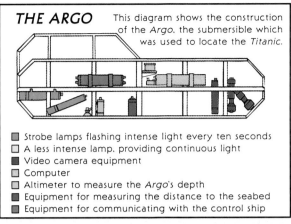

THE ARGO This diagram shows the construction of the *Argo*, the submersible which was used to locate the *Titanic*.

- ☐ Strobe lamps flashing intense light every ten seconds
- ☐ A less intense lamp, providing continuous light
- ■ Video camera equipment
- ☐ Computer
- ☐ Altimeter to measure the *Argo*'s depth
- ■ Equipment for measuring the distance to the seabed
- ■ Equipment for communicating with the control ship

By the time the US team were ready to set off, the French National Institute of Oceanography (IFREMER) was also planning a trip to test search equipment. The two teams joined forces ~ although both hoped that they would be first to spot the *Titanic*.

NO LUCK

In June 1985, the French ship, *Le Suroit*, began to sweep the seabed with an advanced sonar scanner. But rough weather blew the scanner off course. After five weeks, no wreck had been found. In August, the *Argo* was finally lowered into the water from the American research ship *Knorr*.

During two days of filming in an area known as "Titanic Canyon", nothing appeared on the *Argo*'s monitor except fields of mud. Ballard worried that this trip would also be a failure.

CHANGE OF SCENE

The *Knorr* headed for the last unexplored area of the canyon, and searched there for four days with no results.

Then, at 12:40am on September 1, with only five days of the expedition left, something appeared on the monitor screen. It was a massive, round object, surrounded by other pieces of wreckage strewn across the seabed.

Ballard, who had gone to bed, was called from his bunk. As soon as he saw the big round shape, he thought he recognized it. He compared it to one of the pictures he had studied with Bill Tantum, showing the *Titanic*'s massive boilers. The shapes matched exactly: this was the wreck of the *Titanic*.

PICTURES GALORE

Over the next few days, the *Argo* explored the wreck, relaying images of all kinds of wreckage, teacups, wine bottles, chamber pots and dozens of other objects, as the news that the *Titanic* had been found spread quickly around the world.

The tiny submersible *Argo*, attached to the research ship *Knorr* by a cable, explores the wreck of the *Titanic*, nearly 4km (2.5 miles) deep. This picture is drawn to scale.

There is a distance of about 600m (2,000ft) between the two main pieces of hull wreckage on the seabed.

BROUGHT BACK TO LIFE

The video image on the right shows the railings on the bow, or front end, of the *Titanic*, rusty and encrusted with mineral deposits called concretions, but still intact. This part of the ship was featured in the hugely successful 1997 disaster movie, *Titanic*. The film was partly inspired by Ballard's discovery, and used real video footage of the wreck site.

Ballard intended to return to the search site to find out more about the wreck, but he did not want it disturbed by treasure hunters. He saw the *Titanic* as a sacred place, the grave of all those who had drowned there in 1912. After he'd returned to dry land, he told the media that he hoped it would stay that way.

He did return a year later, this time visiting the wreck himself inside a submersible called *Alvin*. He took more photographs, but he still refused to bring any artefacts to the surface, strongly believing that it would be wrong to do so.

In 1987, though, the French IFREMER team, along with an American company called RMS Titanic, Inc., did collect objects from the *Titanic*, using a submersible with a remote-controlled claw. In 1996, RMS Titanic, Inc. even tried to raise part of the ship's hull, but the attempt failed.

So far, only everyday items, including a ship's bell, dishes and a waiter's jacket have been

Cleaned and restored, many of the items retrieved from the *Titanic* look almost as good as new.

retrieved. But their association with the famous, doomed ocean liner makes them incredibly valuable treasures.

THE TOBERMORY GALLEON

A giant Spanish galleon with a crew of 800 was a rare sight in Tobermory, a small town on a Scottish island. The ship continued to fascinate treasure hunters for centuries.

In 1588, King Philip II of Spain decided to invade England. But his convoy of battleships ~ the Spanish Armada ~ was repelled by Elizabeth I's navy, which set fire to most of the Spanish ships. Many of them fled, sailing around the top of Scotland in an attempt to get back to Spain.

One galleon arrived, desperate for shelter, at Tobermory on the Scottish island of Mull. A local chieftain named Maclean made a deal with the Spaniards. He gave them food, water and wood for repairs, in exchange for their help in defeating his enemies.

The galleon intrigued the locals, who thought it was carrying treasure. Then, after six weeks, the ship unexpectedly blew up and sank in the bay. The explosion was probably an accident ~ although some said Maclean's wife, jealous that he was having an affair with a Spanish princess on board, had caused it deliberately.

This map shows the route the Spanish Armada took: from Spain to the south of England, then home by the northern route around Scotland and Ireland.

Soon, attention turned to the treasure that was thought to have sunk with the ship. Local noblemen argued with Scottish kings over who had rights to the Tobermory treasure, and many attempts were made to salvage it from the wreck, but nothing was found.

In 1729, a treasure hunter named Jacob Rowe explored the wreck using a specially designed diving engine (see below). But after trying for two years, he gave up as well.

In the 20th century, interest in the wreck was revived. One team searched from 1903 to 1909, and came up with a candlestick and a broken sword. Then an amateur adventurer, Colonel Foss, spent 25 years dredging the seabed, but got nowhere.

After World War Two, the search started up yet again, this time involving the British navy. But they found nothing much except a small skull, which had probably belonged to a cabin boy.

THE TRUTH AT LAST

In all this time, no one had thought of investigating old Spanish reports. When someone finally did, they found that the ship, the *San Juan de Sicilia*, had been carrying no treasure. Philip II had kept his riches on other galleons in the Armada. The Tobermory galleon had fooled treasure hunters for nearly 400 years.

This is the diving engine invented by Jacob Rowe for investigating shipwrecks. It was very uncomfortable. The diver had to lie inside a curved tube made of copper, with his arms sticking out of two holes.

The two leather sleeves were made to fit the diver's arms exactly, so that they would be watertight.

A glass porthole here allowed the diver to see out.

This lid was screwed tightly in place when the diver was inside.

A line leading to the surface was threaded through a metal ring and dangled near the diver's hands. He could tug on it to call for help.

The diver had to bend his knees into the curved end of the diving engine.

A QUEST FOR PIRATE PLUNDER

For 250 years, the Whydah's pirate treasure lay at the bottom of the Atlantic Ocean, its whereabouts a mystery.

In 1717, the *Whydah* galley sank off Cape Cod, North America, bringing to an end a tale of piracy and treasure. The *Whydah* was a trading ship, but had been captured by the pirate "Black Sam" Bellamy and his men and then used to chase and attack other vessels. The hold was filled with bags of looted valuables. On the night of the sinking, the pirates had captured a ship carrying a cargo of wine, and were all drunk. This, and a storm, took Bellamy and 143 of his crew to a watery grave.

As soon as the governor of Massachusetts heard about the sinking, he sent an officer, Captain Southack, to retrieve as much of the treasure as possible for the government.

But Southack was out of luck. The locals, helped by one of the wreck's two survivors, had already taken some treasure, and they refused to say where they'd put it. Southack eventually gave up, but before he left, he drew several, careful maps of the place where the *Whydah* went down.

The *Whydah*'s treasure stayed under the sea for over 250 years, a source of local folk tales and gossip, until a part-time treasure hunter, called Barry Clifford, decided to search for it.

Clifford studied Captain Southack's maps of the sinking, which he found in the library. Using the maps, he pinpointed the area where he thought the wreck must be. By 1982, he was ready to start looking.

An artist's impression of the *Whydah*'s last moments.

CASH CRISIS

Clifford had a boat, but not much money for equipment. The only thing he could afford was a magnetometer.

On one of his first trips out, the magnetometer gave a response at a site 460m (1500ft) offshore. Clifford was puzzled, as Southack's maps indicated the wreck to be only 150m (500ft) offshore.

He had to investigate ~ but for that, he would need more money. He invited some wealthy businessmen to invest in the chance of "real pirate treasure". They were interested, and Clifford raised a quarter of a million dollars.

Clifford used the money to set up a company, Maritime Explorations. He bought two boats, diving gear, and propwashes ~ machines which can clear mud from the seabed (see page 25).

LACK OF LUCK

With his new equipment and a newly hired crew, Clifford set off to search the seabed. At first, he faced problems ~ one of his new boats was badly damaged when it hit a rock. Looking for the *Whydah* also proved a time-consuming business.

Whenever the magnetometer showed a blip, the spot was marked with a buoy. Propwashes blasted the area and finally, once the sediment had settled, divers went down to investigate. But time after time, they surfaced with nothing.

WRECKED HOPES

By the summer of 1984, things were going really badly. The team had found no treasure, Clifford was running out of money to pay his crew, and he was wondering whether to give up. Just then, a TV crew arrived, wanting to film the treasure hunters at work.

BACK TO SQUARE ONE

Clifford had no treasure to show the film makers, so, at a crew member's suggestion, he took them back to the site 460m (1500ft) offshore where his magnetometer had first made a blip. Although he had already searched and found nothing there, his propwashes had blasted a vast hole, which would at least give the cameramen something to film.

This time, however, when divers went down to the seabed, they did find something sticking out of the sides of the propwash pit. When Clifford dived in to join them, he saw three cannon muzzles in the mud, covered with concretions ~ a crusty coating of minerals and sand. With a storm brewing, he barely had time to grab a grapefruit-sized lump from the seabed before heading back up to the boat.

Barry Clifford checking Captain Southack's maps on the shore of Cape Cod. His first estimate of the site of the *Whydah* failed to take into account the slow movement of the coastline over hundreds of years.

MAP MISTAKE

Back on board, Clifford picked off the crust surrounding the lump. It concealed a blackened coin ~ a silver Spanish piece of eight, dated 1684. He realized he had probably found the *Whydah* at last. But how could it be so far away from the site described by Captain Southack's maps?

Suddenly, Clifford realized he had made a mistake. Over the centuries that had passed since the sinking, the coastline would have eroded and changed, thus altering the coordinates.

TREASURE TROVE

Whether or not the wreck was the *Whydah*, it produced plenty of treasure. On the first day of diving alone, the crew brought up over a thousand gold and silver coins.

Obeying instructions from the state, Clifford hired an archaeologist to carry out a survey on the site. A laboratory was set up on the search ship, and each find was logged on a computer. In a couple of months, divers brought up 7,310 valuable items. But there was still no way of proving that the ship was Sam Bellamy's pirate vessel.

When the divers found a large, rounded object in the mud, Clifford recognized it as a bell.

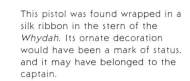

This pistol was found wrapped in a silk ribbon in the stern of the *Whydah*. Its ornate decoration would have been a mark of status, and it may have belonged to the captain.

He knew that most ship's bells had the name of the ship engraved on them. It took three weeks to loosen the concretions coating the bell; but at last they were chipped away, to reveal the inscription, "1716 THE WHYDAH GALLY". (*Gally* is another way to spell "galley".)

Clifford was now able to repay his backers and build a museum to display some of the treasure preserved from the *Whydah*, said to be worth $400 million (£250 million).

A PIRATE'S LIFE

Life as a pirate was hard, despite the lure of easy money. Long months at sea, perilous weather, and the threat of execution for pirates who got caught made for a difficult existence.

Nevertheless, in the early 1700s piracy flourished. Sailors who had left the navy, criminals in search of a quick fortune, merchants who had fallen on hard times, and escaped slaves all thought the risks worth taking. This continued until the mid-1700s, when piracy was so widespread that European navies took action and hunted the pirates down.

This picture shows an artist's impression of "Black Sam" Bellamy, pirate captain of the *Whydah* when it sank in 1717.

CHINA CARGO

Although the Dutch trading ship the Geldermalsen *did have some gold on board, its cargo of inexpensive china was the most valuable find for treasure hunters.*

In 1751, the Dutch trading ship the *Geldermalsen* was in Canton (now Guangzhou), China, loading up with goods for the journey home. Its main cargo was tea, for which there was a huge demand in Europe. The height of fashion was to drink it out of "Nanking" china from Canton; and over 200 crates of this blue and white porcelain were packed underneath the tea in the ship's hold.

The china was mass-produced and not very high-quality, but it has since become very valuable to collectors. As well as tea services, there were bowls, models of people and animals, cups and saucers and even vomit pots, which people used if they ate too much during a heavy meal.

In the 18th century, Canton, which is now known as Guangzhou, was a thriving port visited by ships from all over the world.

In late December 1751, the ship set off across the South China Sea. A few days later, on January 3, disaster struck. The boatswain reported that the ship had safely passed the dangerous Admiral Stellingwerf Reef, but he was wrong.

That evening, they hit the reef. At first the ship seemed to have survived but during the night it started to sink, and 80 of the 112 passengers and crew on board drowned.

The precious cargo was also lost and the value of Nanking china shot up back home in the Netherlands.

EASTERN TRADE

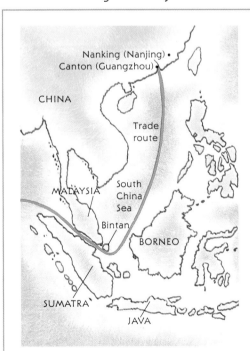

The map on the left shows the route 18th-century trading vessels took from China to Europe with their cargoes of tea, silk, porcelain, gold, gemstones and spices such as pepper and cloves.

Unless they went the long way around past Java, they had to pass through the narrow straits between Malaysia and Sumatra, where dangerous reefs, like the Admiral Stellingwerf, regularly caused shipwrecks.

Chinese tea, silk, gems and porcelain were highly prized by 18th-century Europeans.

The *Geldermalsen* lay at the bottom of the sea for over 200 years, while Nanking china gradually increased in value. Anyone who could find the 239,000 pieces of sunken crockery would surely make a fortune. Eventually, in 1983, a treasure salvager named Michael Hatcher headed for the area with a team of divers, hoping to locate the wreck.

JUNK

After only a few days, the divers found pieces of porcelain on the seabed near the spot where the *Geldermalsen* had gone down. But this wasn't Nanking china. Instead, they had discovered the wreck of a 17th-century junk, a Chinese trading ship, which had been carrying rare porcelain from the Ming period. After retrieving the china, Hatcher sold it at auction. It raised £2 million ($3 million), enough to fund a second search for the *Geldermalsen*.

EXPERT ADVICE

This time, Hatcher used the expertise of Max de Rham, a marine surveyor. De Rham advised using a magnetometer and sonar scanner to find objects on the seabed. In March 1985, they set off again for the South China Sea.

On the very first day with the new equipment, Hatcher's team found two large anchors, but nothing

A crate of the *Geldermalsen*'s cargo being raised from the seabed.

else turned up for two months. Then, on May 12, the divers found a hole in the seabed. It contained another anchor, cannons, and several oddly shaped lumps. When taken to the surface and cleaned, they turned out to be blue and white porcelain: the Nanking china.

Hatcher used an airlift, a machine which sucks mud up from the seabed, to expose the wreck. Soon the crates full of china were visible, with the tightly packed tea congealed on top of them.

For weeks, the divers worked constantly.

Getting the china out of the crates meant disturbing the tea leaves, which escaped into the water. Hatcher said it was like working inside a giant teapot.

In June, there was one final surprise. A diver came to the surface with a handful of small, curved gold ingots shaped like shoes, a Chinese symbol of wealth. Altogether 109 ingots were found.

CHINA SALE

In 1986, a year after the *Geldermalsen* was found, its cargo was auctioned in Amsterdam for £16 million ($25 million). Most of it went to wealthy collectors, but ordinary people, intrigued by the story of this delicate cargo, were able to afford Nanking cups and saucers to commemorate the discovery.

The pattern on this teacup and saucer was typical of Nanking china. Look out for it in museums.

ARCTIC EXPEDITION

This World War Two treasure was only 40 years old, but worth so much that treasure hunters competed to be allowed to retrieve it.

During World War Two, one of the most important ~ and dangerous ~ sea routes was the one between Russia and Britain, around the top of Scandinavia. It was vital for Britain to ship tanks, guns and other supplies to its ally, Russia, along this route. But any vessel making the trip risked being attacked by German ships or U-boats (submarines). There was also a danger of sinking under the weight of ice that gathered on the ship's structure in the freezing conditions.

PERILOUS JOURNEY

In April 1942, the giant warship *HMS Edinburgh* set out from Murmansk, Russia, to make the perilous trip. A convoy of supply ships had just delivered a consignment of weapons to Russia, and the *Edinburgh* was to accompany them home, clearing a path through the ice floes and guarding against German attack. The *Edinburgh* was also carrying a precious cargo.

The sailors had loaded on board 93 small wooden boxes which held cans of beans for the home journey ~ or so they were told. In fact, the boxes hid 465 solid gold ingots: part of Russia's payment for the war supplies it had received.

ATTACK!

The Germans didn't know about the gold but they had seen the convoy and planned an attack. On April 30, just a day after the ship had set sail, two torpedoes from a U-boat ploughed into the *Edinburgh*'s stern, destroying the steering system. Several men were killed and many more were injured. The ship could no longer steer properly, so it limped around in circles, unable to escape.

The map shows the route the search ship *Dammtor* took from its base in Peterhead, Scotland, to the *Edinburgh*'s wreck site.

This type of watch, called a deck watch, was standard Royal Navy issue and would have been used by a sailor on board *HMS Edinburgh*. It shows the time the ship was hit by the first torpedo: 4:18pm.

Six forward-facing gun turrets

Equipment for launching aircraft from the deck

The steel sides of *HMS Edinburgh* were 8-11.5cm (3-4¼in) thick.

CLOSING IN

On May 2, German submarines and battleships surrounded the crippled ship, bombarding it with torpedoes and gunfire. Hundreds of sailors were evacuated onto two other ships in the convoy as the *Edinburgh* began to tilt dangerously.

The ship did not go down, however, and the British were worried that if it stayed afloat the Germans might go on board and find the gold. In the end, it was a British torpedo that sank the *Edinburgh* ~ to make sure the secret cargo would not fall into enemy hands.

WAR GRAVE

The Russian gold was not forgotten. There were plans to salvage it; but this would be difficult as the treasure lay 245m (800ft) deep and was encased in the *Edinburgh*'s thick steel hull. Then, in 1957, the wreck site was named an official war grave. This meant plans which had involved blasting into the ship to reach the gold had to be abandoned.

NEW PLANS

By the 1970s, however, the British government was anxious to retrieve the treasure. Otherwise it might be stolen by pirates, or collected by the Russians themselves, now Britain's enemies in the Cold War.

A diver named Keith Jessop came up with a salvage plan. He had worked on North Sea oil rigs, using heavy underwater cutting equipment at great depths. He thought this technology could also be used on *HMS Edinburgh*, thus avoiding the need for explosives. Using divers instead calmed the British government's fears of disturbing a war grave.

SHIP AHOY

In 1981, Jessop's company, Jessop Marine, won the contract, and work began. First of all, Jessop had to locate the wreck. His search ship, the *Dammtor*, set off from Peterhead in Scotland, carrying a range of hi-tech equipment for scanning the seabed.

Just 15 days later, the *Dammtor*'s sonar scanning device picked up the image of a huge wreck on the ocean floor. A remote-controlled underwater vehicle was lowered into the water to explore the site. When fuzzy pictures of the *Edinburgh*'s gun turrets appeared on the monitors in the control room, they knew they'd found the right wreck.

HMS Harrier, on the left, lies alongside *HMS Edinburgh* as crew members from the stricken ship are evacuated.

HMS Edinburgh had six guns facing out to each side.

Six backward-facing gun turrets

DEEP-SEA DANGERS

Deep-sea diving is an extremely hazardous occupation. The deeper a diver goes, the greater the water pressure becomes. At high pressures, the gases that the diver breathes, such as oxygen, get compressed. This means that more gas than usual is dissolved in the bloodstream.

If the pressure is then reduced too quickly, for example by rising to the surface too fast, bubbles of gas can form in the blood. This leads to an often deadly condition known as "the bends".

AVOIDING THE BENDS

To be safe from the bends, divers must readjust to normal air pressure very slowly. When Jessop's divers returned to the surface after a deep dive, they stayed in a sealed compression chamber on the ship. The air pressure in the chamber was the same as the water pressure on the seabed. When the expedition ended, the pressure in the chamber was slowly reduced over several days, allowing the divers to adjust gradually.

OPERATION GREYHOUND

After finding the wreck, the next step was to cut open the *Edinburgh*'s hull to find the gold. For this, Jessop needed a different ship ~ his salvage ship, the *Stephaniturm* ~ and a team of specially chosen divers. He returned to Peterhead to make arrangements.

The project was named Operation Greyhound, and security was very tight. If the mission was successful, the returning *Stephaniturm*, loaded with gold, could easily be attacked. It was agreed that all communications to and from the ship would be in code, and that every stage of the operation would be filmed.

FIRST STRIKE

The *Stephaniturm* and her crew set off on August 30, 1981, and the first dive took place on September 4. Three divers sat inside a diving bell which was lowered onto the seabed through a hole, called a moon-pool, in the bottom of the salvage ship.

PRESSURE SHOCK

But when they reached the depths, the divers realized they were not ready. Simply moving around under the pressure of such deep water was exhausting, and they had no energy to carry out the heavy cutting work. They had to return to the surface and prepare more slowly, building up their strength and getting used to the water pressure.

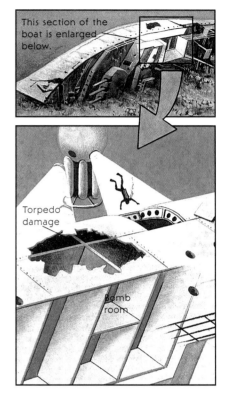

This section of the boat is enlarged below.

Torpedo damage

Bomb room

Unable to reach the gold through the hole made by the torpedo, the divers cut a new hole in the hull of the *Edinburgh*, which lay on its side on the seabed.

A HOLE IN THE HULL

Eventually, the divers adjusted to the conditions. From the *Stephaniturm*'s control room, Jessop was able to communicate with them as they worked, using a radio link. Painstakingly, the divers cut their way through to the room which stored the treasure. For the entire time, they were in danger of being crushed by falling debris.

Finally, after nine days of work, a piece of the *Edinburgh*'s hull was lifted clear of the wreckage. Excited, the team took photographs of the hull before returning it to the water. Now they could explore inside the ship and search for the missing treasure.

But just over a week later, the divers were running out of willpower. Several of them had bad ear infections, and burns caused by the hot water which circulated in their diving suits to prevent them from freezing.

PAYBACK

It wasn't until September 16, that diver John Rossier, clearing debris from the bomb room, came across a strange metal block ~ strange in that it was heavier than the others he had found. His cry of "I've found the gold!" blasted across the control room on board the *Stephaniturm*.

It took 20 minutes for a salvage crate to lift the precious discovery to the surface. When it arrived, Jessop cleaned it and uncovered the imprint "KPO620" ~ a Russian serial number.

The first gold bar to be raised from the depths was scrubbed clean with soapy water to reveal a serial number and the Russian hammer and sickle symbol.

TIME TO GO

Over the next three weeks, the team of divers managed to retrieve most of the *HMS Edinburgh's* 465 gold bars. These were carefully cleaned and locked into a safe on board. But winter was closing in, and bad weather threatened the salvage operation. The divers were exhausted and ill, and Jessop was worried this might cause an accident. In the end, they decided to head for home, leaving 34 gold bars behind. Jessop resolving to return for them another day.

JESSOP'S SHARE

The 431 gold bars retrieved from *HMS Edinburgh* were safely carried back to Britain. The value of the haul was over £43 million ($65 million). This was finally split between the British and Russian governments, Keith Jessop's company, Jessop Marine, and the financial backers who had supported him. Jessop himself made around £2 million ($3 million), while each of the divers was paid around £30,000 ($45,000).

Keith Jessop   4.5%

Financial backers
40.5%

Russian government
37.22%

British government
17.78%

ANCIENT TREASURE

Like the buried treasures at the beginning of this book, the oldest treasure of all is usually underground. This is partly because being buried, especially in certain types of clay or sand, can preserve objects ~ and bodies ~ that would otherwise have rotted or rusted away.

Much of this treasure is found in tombs, where it was placed alongside the bodies of monarchs and aristocrats to make sure they were well-provided for in the next life. Often, ancient people preserved the body itself for the same reason ~ so that the dead person wouldn't go through the next life with only a skeleton.

Preserved dead bodies are valuable to historians, as they can tell us about how people lived, but graves must be treated with respect. After investigation, the dead person is usually returned to the coffin and reburied.

CITY TREASURE

Some treasures, such as the remains of the city of Troy, are not tombs. Troy was underground because many cities had been built on top of it. Also, over the centuries, ruined buildings fall down, to be covered by soil and vegetation. They must be excavated by trained scientists who know how to protect what they find.

Ancient treasure is often amazingly beautiful, made of solid gold, silver and gemstones and decorated by skilled craftsmen. But even everyday objects from ancient sites are precious, because of their rarity and historical value.

46

THE PHARAOH'S TOMB

After years of searching, Howard Carter was rewarded by the sight of roomfuls of treasure in the tomb of a murdered ancient Egyptian king.

The map of Egypt above shows the Valley of the Kings, where Tutankhamun and many other pharaohs were buried in treasure-filled tombs.

Howard Carter, on the right, and Lord Carnarvon, in hats to protect them from the fierce Egyptian sun.

Tutankhamun was only a child when he became pharaoh (king of Egypt) in about 1333BC. He ruled for ten years, but was probably controlled by two older men, Ay and Horemheb. They were trying to reinstate the old gods, banned by the previous pharaoh, Akhenaten. He had believed in worshipping only the sun, or "Aten", and had destroyed all the old temples. It was a turbulent time in Egyptian history, and experts think that when Tutankhamun died, aged only 18, he was almost certainly murdered.

ON THE TRAIL OF A TOMB

Tutankhamun wasn't a very important ruler while he was alive, but, like other pharaohs of the period, he was buried in a grand tomb, surrounded by precious statues, gold and jewels.

Over 3,000 years later, an English archaeologist named Howard Carter set out to search for it. Carter had previously worked as an inspector of historical sites in Egypt, where many tombs had already been found. Tutankhamun's had not yet been discovered and Carter was determined to find it.

A FLIGHT OF STEPS

Carter spent several years scouring the Valley of the Kings, near Luxor in eastern Egypt, for the tomb. He was financed by his friend Lord Carnarvon, an English aristocrat ~ but by 1922, Carnarvon was worried. Would he ever see a result from all the money he had poured into Carter's scheme? Carter persuaded him to fund one last search, and on the morning of November 4, 1922, he was amazed to find his workmen standing quietly, staring at a single stone step half-buried in the sand.

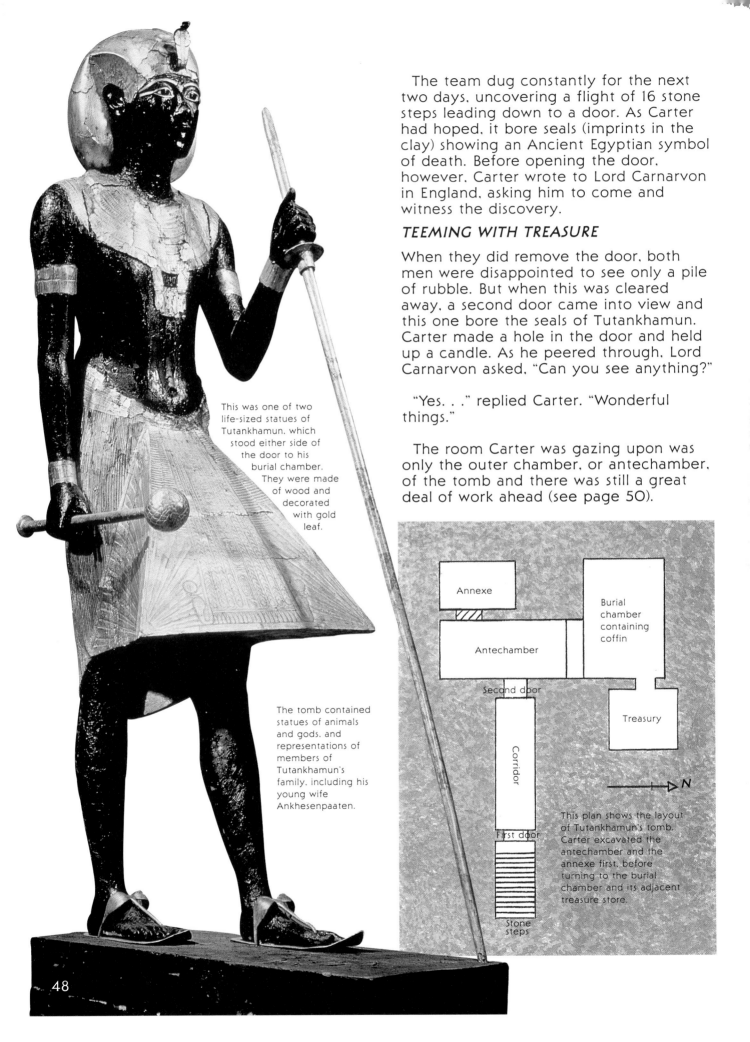

The team dug constantly for the next two days, uncovering a flight of 16 stone steps leading down to a door. As Carter had hoped, it bore seals (imprints in the clay) showing an Ancient Egyptian symbol of death. Before opening the door, however, Carter wrote to Lord Carnarvon in England, asking him to come and witness the discovery.

TEEMING WITH TREASURE

When they did remove the door, both men were disappointed to see only a pile of rubble. But when this was cleared away, a second door came into view and this one bore the seals of Tutankhamun. Carter made a hole in the door and held up a candle. As he peered through, Lord Carnarvon asked, "Can you see anything?"

"Yes. . ." replied Carter. "Wonderful things."

The room Carter was gazing upon was only the outer chamber, or antechamber, of the tomb and there was still a great deal of work ahead (see page 50).

This was one of two life-sized statues of Tutankhamun, which stood either side of the door to his burial chamber. They were made of wood and decorated with gold leaf.

The tomb contained statues of animals and gods, and representations of members of Tutankhamun's family, including his young wife Ankhesenpaaten.

Annexe

Burial chamber containing coffin

Antechamber

Second door

Treasury

Corridor

N

First door

This plan shows the layout of Tutankhamun's tomb. Carter excavated the antechamber and the annexe first, before turning to the burial chamber and its adjacent treasure store.

Stone steps

48

INSIDE THE BURIAL CHAMBER

   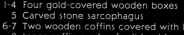 

1-4 Four gold-covered wooden boxes
5   Carved stone sarcophagus
6-7 Two wooden coffins covered with beaten gold
8   Inner coffin made of solid gold
9   Mummified body and death mask

1   2   3   4   5   6   7   8 9

When Carter finally opened the inner chamber, he found a huge wooden box covered with gold. It almost filled the room. The golden box held three more, each one inside the one before. Inside the fourth was a sarcophagus, or stone coffin, covered in carvings. Inside that was a wooden coffin covered with beaten gold and decorated with precious stones, with another similar coffin inside it. The final, inner coffin was made of solid gold, down to the nails which held the lid in place, and inlaid with precious jewels.

A BODY AT LAST

When his workmen finally lifted away the coffin lid, Carter saw the linen wrappings and thick ointments that had been used to preserve, or mummify, the young pharaoh's body. As the layers of cloth were peeled away, over 140 trinkets and jewels were found among them, placed there to help the king in his new life.

Carter also discovered that the body was wearing a death mask. This was a lifelike copy of the young man's face, cast in solid gold and inlaid with precious blue stones called obsidian and lapis lazuli. This famous mask has since become one of the best-known archaeological finds of all time.

The golden inner coffin of Tutankhamun's tomb, with its rich, detailed decoration; and the linen-wrapped, mummified body which lay hidden beneath

49

CARTER'S METHODS

Carter was a conscientious archaeologist who took his responsibilities seriously. He was careful to document and preserve everything taken from the tomb. Each item was given a numbered label showing its place in the tomb, and the objects were also photographed in position before being moved.

Many items were moved to a laboratory to be repaired and preserved. Small objects were carried in boxes, larger ones on padded stretchers. Carter used an empty tomb at the far end of the Valley of the Kings as a laboratory, as it was cool and spacious and could be guarded against robbers.

These rings from the tomb were meticulously drawn by Carter to record their details.

After Carter's first glimpse through the outer door of the tomb, he widened the hole and shone a flashlight inside. The room glittered with gold. A gilded throne carved into animal shapes threw strange shadows, and gems winked in the light. To the right of the chamber was a doorway, guarded by two life-sized models of Tutankhamun. Carter guessed this was the entrance to the burial chamber itself.

THE NEWS SPREADS

The story of the amazing discovery soon spread around the world and reporters flocked to the site. But before Carter would open the inner tomb, he insisted on dealing with the contents of the outer chamber. Over three months, he marked, listed and stored every object he found there, including statues, weapons, chariots, ornaments, vases and jewels.

KING TUT FEVER

Meanwhile, the world was going Tutankhamun-mad. Visiting the tomb became the height of fashion, with tourists arriving in hordes and celebrities posing for photographs by the entrance. New ranges of clothes came out, based on Ancient Egyptian designs. People wore gemstones based on the tomb's treasures. Some women even wore layers of cloth wrapped around themselves, like Egyptian mummies.

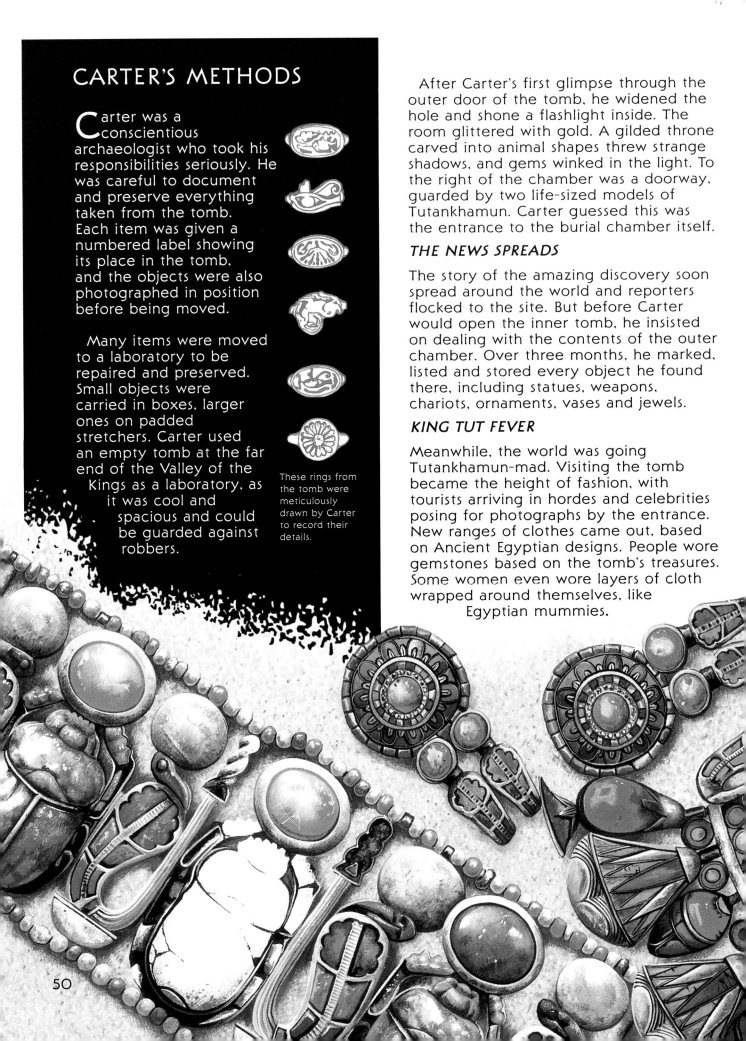

Carter took so long to open the burial chamber that some frustrated journalists began to make up stories, claiming that there was a curse on the tomb. In one version, Carter was supposed to have secretly removed a stone tablet from the chamber, bearing the scary message: "*Death will slay with his wings whoever disturbs the pharaoh's peace.*" The press grew even wilder when a "lucky" canary belonging to Carter was eaten by a cobra.

THE CHAMBER IS OPENED

At last, Carter was ready to open the inner chamber. Historians and officials gathered to watch as he broke open the door. Inside he found the first of the gold-covered wooden boxes which would later reveal the pharaoh's body (see page 49). But to everyone's frustration, the work was postponed because of the unbearably hot weather.

A short time later, Lord Carnarvon died in Cairo from an infected mosquito bite, fuelling rumours about a curse. Carter ignored them, upset only by the fact that his friend would now never know whether the tomb really did contain Tutankhamun's body. It was only in October 1925, that the inner coffin containing the mummified body was opened.

MUMMIFYING A BODY

The Ancient Egyptians believed that death was a gateway to a new life, and that dead bodies had to be preserved for use in the next world. This was done using a process called mummification.

A dead person's mourners had to make sure the body was preserved as soon as possible.

All the internal organs were removed from the body and put in pots called canopic jars. The body was left to dry out in a container filled with a salt called natron.

Canopic jars

Wrapping the body

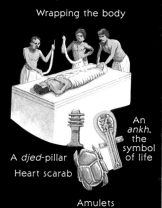

The body cavity was then packed with natron and resin. The face was painted and the entire body was embalmed (smeared with preserving ointments) and wrapped up in linen strips. Amulets (lucky charms) were placed between each layer.

A *djed*-pillar
Heart scarab

An *ankh*, the symbol of life

Amulets

The whole process took around 70 days, after which a funeral was held. Poor people were buried in the sand, but the wealthier members of society were sealed inside several coffins and buried in tombs cut out of rock.

The chief embalmer wore a jackal mask to represent Anubis, the patron god of embalmers.

Hundreds of fabulous jewels were among the treasures found in Tutankhamun's tomb. The large bracelet on the left was found on the right arm of the mummified body. The earrings were in a small jewel box in the treasury. The item on the right is called a pectoral, designed to be hung around the neck.

THE JADE PUZZLE

Instead of a body, archaeologists at the tomb of Prince Lui Sheng found a jigsaw puzzle: the pieces of jade that had made up the prince's burial suit.

In 1968, soldiers patrolling Lingshan Mountain in Hebei Province, Northeast China, found a strange underground tunnel. They squeezed inside and, to their amazement, saw rows of glinting pots, statues and vases. Experts soon identified it as the long-lost tomb of Prince Lui Sheng, who had ruled the Beijing area from 154-113BC.

INSIDE THE TOMB

Near Prince Lui Sheng's tomb, investigators found that of his wife, Dou Wan. Both tombs were huge, and must have taken many years to carve out of the rock.

In the outer chambers, archaeologists found jewels, fine silk and ornaments cut from jade, a precious green stone. They also discovered ten chariots and the skeletons of thirty horses, which had been sacrificed and buried with the prince.

A TOMB WITHOUT A BODY

The archaeologists finally reached the inner chamber, where they expected to find the body of Prince Lui Sheng. But when they heaved open the doors, they saw no coffin and no body. Instead, thousands of slivers of jade lay on a table, among countless tiny strands of fine gold wire. The same scene awaited them in Dou Wan's chamber.

PRESERVING POWER

The Ancient Chinese believed that jade had magical properties, and could preserve bodies forever. To keep them fresh for the afterlife, Lui Sheng and his wife had been encased in suits made entirely of small pieces of jade, held together with gold thread. These suits are called *yu-xia*. Although they had fallen apart, most of the pieces were intact, and the archaeologists planned to attempt to fit the suits back together.

The 2,498 pieces of jade that had made up Lui Sheng's suit were lifted onto a flat, metal grid.

Fine gold wires were threaded through tiny holes made with a high-precision drill.

Dou Wan's suit was more badly damaged, so each one of its 2,160 pieces was photographed and given a number. A 3-D computer image was made, matching the jade pieces to the shape of a body.

The archaeologists estimated that each suit would have taken craftsmen over ten years of skilled work to complete. But, although Lui Sheng's suit survived for over 2,000 years, only a few teeth were left of the prince himself.

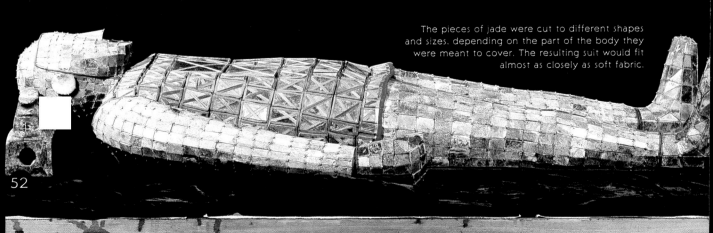

The pieces of jade were cut to different shapes and sizes, depending on the part of the body they were meant to cover. The resulting suit would fit almost as closely as soft fabric.

AN UNDERGROUND ARMY

Hundreds of individual clay soldiers guard the tomb of China's first emperor, which has still not been opened.

In March 1974, Chinese peasants digging a hole for a well discovered a hollow pit. Peering inside, they came face to face with a life-sized soldier, made out of a red clay called terracotta. He was the first of hundreds: the farmers had found a terracotta army.

Archaeologists explored the site and found a huge underground cavern, full of soldiers lined up in battle formation. Studying objects from the site gave them an explanation. The soldiers were guarding the tomb of Huang Di, the first Chinese emperor and the builder of the Great Wall of China.

Huang Di was terrified of dying. He had searched in vain for the secret of eternal life, and decided that if he could not be immortal, he would at least have a magnificent tomb. Ancient accounts say his burial chamber had a ceiling studded with gems, and a model of his vast empire, with rivers made of mercury. Crossbows were set to fire automatically on intruders.

SKELETONS

As well as two more pits full of clay horses and soldiers, the tomb contained real skeletons: some of rare birds and animals, and some of the slaves who had built the tomb, beheaded and still wearing leg-irons. They had been murdered after their work was done, to make sure the tomb's location stayed a secret.

The burial chamber itself is still unopened. Experts say they want to wait until technology can preserve what might be inside.

The terracotta army was designed to scare robbers and intruders away from an imperial tomb. But the soldiers' artistic value, age and rarity make them treasures in themselves.

Each terracotta soldier has his own individual features and facial expression.

THE MARCHIONESS OF DA

The beautifully preserved body of an aristocratic lady lay at the heart of a complicated tomb, consisting of layer upon layer of coffins.

In 1971, plans for a hospital in the Hunang Province in southeast China, were interrupted when the surveyors realized that the new building would encroach on an ancient burial mound. The archaeologists who were sent to investigate didn't expect to find much. They thought grave robbers would have long since stolen anything of value.

When they had dug 15m (50ft) underground, however, they discovered a sloping ramp. This led to a burial chamber, lined with thick layers of clay and charcoal ~ a method often used by the Ancient Chinese to keep burial chambers dry.

A NEST OF COFFINS

Inside the chamber, the archaeologists found a large wooden coffin,

which was also lined with charcoal. Inside this was a second, decorated coffin made of black cypress wood and containing vases, rolls of silks, exquisite ornaments ~ and another coffin.

On and on the experts went, unpacking coffin after coffin, five in all, each one nestling inside the one before, like a set of Russian dolls.

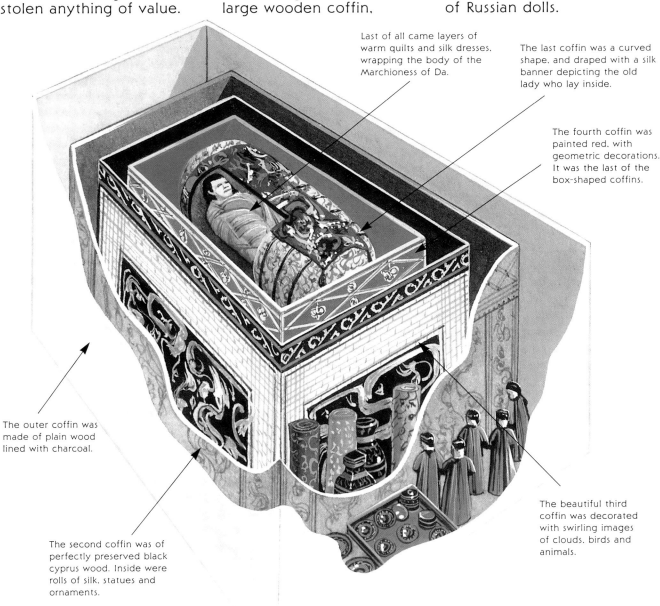

Last of all came layers of warm quilts and silk dresses, wrapping the body of the Marchioness of Da.

The last coffin was a curved shape, and draped with a silk banner depicting the old lady who lay inside.

The fourth coffin was painted red, with geometric decorations. It was the last of the box-shaped coffins.

The outer coffin was made of plain wood lined with charcoal.

The second coffin was of perfectly preserved black cyprus wood. Inside were rolls of silk, statues and ornaments.

The beautiful third coffin was decorated with swirling images of clouds, birds and animals.

Plates containing 2,000-year-old morsels of food were found in the tomb. These were intended for the Marchioness to use in her afterlife.

A COFFIN WITH A CLUE

The fifth and final coffin was different from the others. Instead of being box-shaped, it was rounded and curved to the shape of a human body. Draped over the top of it was a T-shaped, hand-painted silk banner. It showed an elderly lady, surrounded by servants and friends, preparing for a glorious afterlife. The banner seemed to tell the story of the last days of the tomb's occupant.

WELL-DRESSED CORPSE

When this coffin was opened, it contained a bulky shape clothed in many layers of fabric. Carefully, archaeologists unwrapped 20 quilts and numerous layers of fine silk dresses.

At the heart of the bundle lay a plump, middle-aged woman. Her skin was still soft and her features clear. She even had her mouth open as if she was snoring in her sleep.

A GRAND LADY

Records buried with the body stated that the lady was a Marchioness ~ the wife of a type of ruler called a Marquis. Her husband had been the Marquis of Da, a wealthy Chinese aristocrat who lived during the 2nd century BC.

HER LAST MEAL

Tests and forensic studies followed. A medical examination of the body, even though it was conducted over 2,000 years after her death, was able to reveal that the Marchioness had died from a heart attack. The investigation also found that she had just eaten a watermelon. Scientists discovered 138 whole seeds still in her stomach.

STOPPING THE ROT

Unlike jade, which was wrongly believed to preserve bodies, charcoal and clay really did. The suits made for Prince Lui Sheng and his wife (see page 52) didn't preserve them at all, but the clay and charcoal around the Marchioness kept her body fresh. They also did an excellent job of preserving the coffins and their contents.

IN SEARCH OF LEGENDS

An eight-year quest for the mythical cities of Mycenae and Troy led to some amazing discoveries, and some embarrassing mistakes.

Troy is famed in legend as a city of glorious wealth and power. But did it really exist? In the 1860s, Heinrich Schliemann, a millionaire German businessman, decided to find out.

The city of Troy and its location were described by the Greek poet Homer, in his poem *The Iliad*, which told the story of the Trojan War (c. 1250BC). Schliemann was convinced that the place Homer described was now a scrub-covered hillside in Turkey.

The map shows present-day Greece and Turkey, which were the homes of two warring sides in Ancient Greek legend, and the starting point for Schliemann's quest for the treasures of their mythical kings.

In 1872, after obtaining permission from the Turkish government, Schliemann hired 80 men and set them to work digging up the hillside at Hisarlik, in northwestern Turkey, where he believed Troy had been.

It soon turned out that many cities had been built on the same site over the thousands of years since Troy had stood. Workers cast aside layer upon layer of objects, including pots, weapons, and even human bones, in their search for the city of Troy.

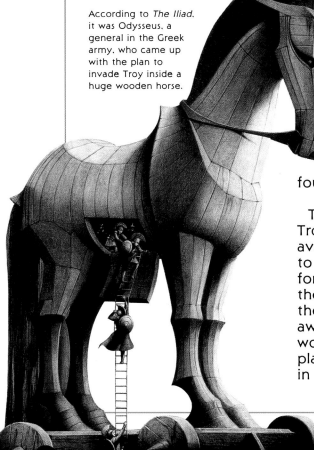

According to *The Iliad*, it was Odysseus, a general in the Greek army, who came up with the plan to invade Troy inside a huge wooden horse.

THE SIEGE OF TROY

Homer's epic poem *The Iliad* tells how the Trojans kidnapped Helen, beautiful sister-in-law of Agamemnon, a Greek king, and how the Greeks fought to win her back.

The Greeks besieged Troy for ten years, to no avail. Then they decided to use cunning instead of force. They pretended they had given up, and the Greek ships sailed away, leaving a giant wooden horse on the plain outside Troy, as if in offering to their gods.

But the horse was hollow, and packed with Greek soldiers. As the Greeks had hoped, the unwitting Trojans dragged the horse inside the city to offer to their own gods. At long last, the Greeks were within the walls of Troy.

That night, the soldiers crept out of the horse and opened the gates to the rest of their army, who had secretly sailed back. The Greeks then raided the city, rescued Helen and turned triumphantly for home, burning Troy to the ground as they left.

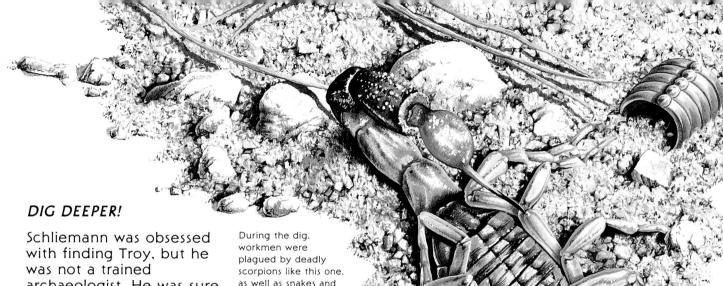

DIG DEEPER!

Schliemann was obsessed with finding Troy, but he was not a trained archaeologist. He was sure Troy was the earliest city on the site, and would be found at the very bottom. He discarded the everyday objects his workmen turned up, believing that when they reached Troy itself, it would be full of spectacular treasures.

DISCOVERING TREASURE

Then, in early June, workmen found a beautiful stone sculpture of the Greek sun god Helios. This proved that at least one important city had stood on the site. Finally, almost a year later, in 1873, Schliemann found what he was looking for.

Digging at the bottom of a ruined wall, he uncovered a copper shield and cauldron, a pair of silver vases and, most impressive of all, a two-handled jug made of solid gold.

In a couple more hours of feverish digging, Schliemann found hundreds of gold earrings and other jewels and ornaments. He believed he had at last unearthed the treasures of Priam, King of Troy.

During the dig, workmen were plagued by deadly scorpions like this one, as well as snakes and other dangerous animals.

SEARCHING FOR AGAMEMNON

Triumphant over his success at Hisarlik, Schliemann headed for Mycenae in Greece. This was the legendary home of Agamemnon, the king whose army had besieged Troy.

According to legend, Agamemnon had been murdered on his return from Troy by his wife and her new lover. Schliemann was determined to find the king's grave, and the rich treasures that he was sure would have been buried with him.

RUTHLESS DESTRUCTION

But in their search for objects from Agamemnon's time, Schliemann's workers smashed through dozens of Greek and Roman remains. This horrified a Greek archaeologist, Stamatkis, who had been hired to advise Schliemann on the project.

As a media stunt, Schliemann had his Greek wife, Sophia, pose for photographs wearing some of the jewels he had found at Hisarlik. He called them "Helen's jewels".

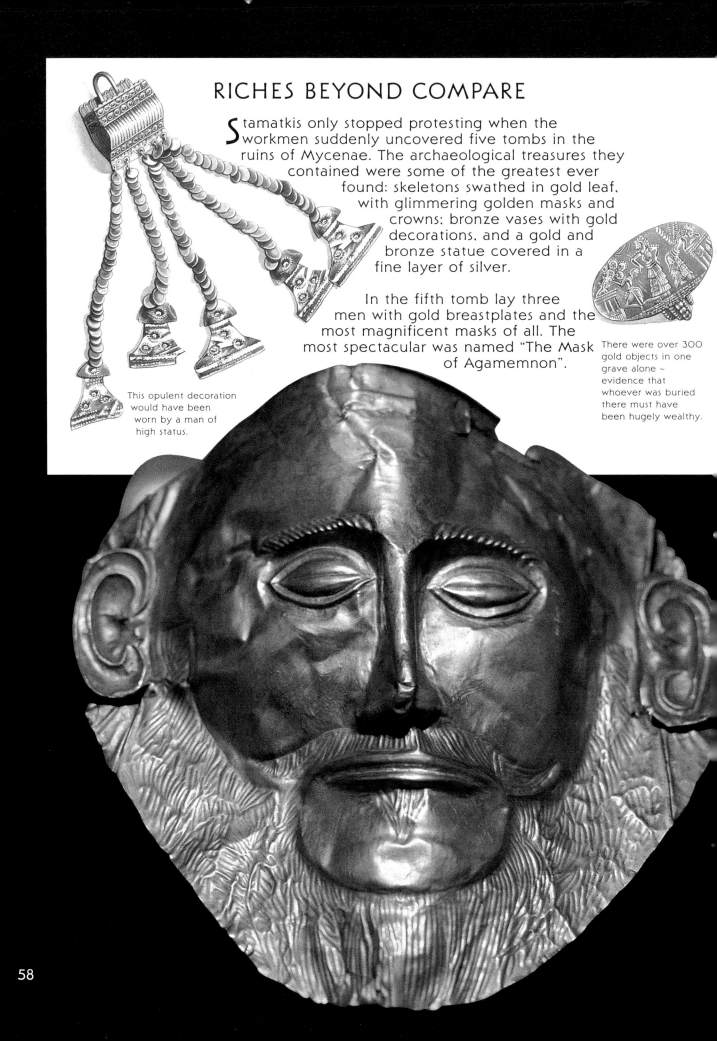

RICHES BEYOND COMPARE

Stamatkis only stopped protesting when the workmen suddenly uncovered five tombs in the ruins of Mycenae. The archaeological treasures they contained were some of the greatest ever found: skeletons swathed in gold leaf, with glimmering golden masks and crowns; bronze vases with gold decorations, and a gold and bronze statue covered in a fine layer of silver.

In the fifth tomb lay three men with gold breastplates and the most magnificent masks of all. The most spectacular was named "The Mask of Agamemnon".

This opulent decoration would have been worn by a man of high status.

There were over 300 gold objects in one grave alone ~ evidence that whoever was buried there must have been hugely wealthy.

58

SCHLIEMANN'S SLIP-UPS

Schliemann had apparently triumphed again. However, his lack of archaeological training and historical knowledge had led him to make a mistake. The body in the fifth tomb was not Agamemnon, but that of an unknown warrior who had been buried centuries before him.

Recent scientific research has revealed an even worse mistake arising from the methods Schliemann used during the excavations at Troy. In his enthusiasm,

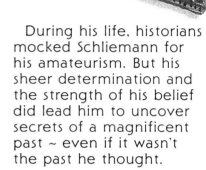

Some of the amazing burial gifts found in the tombs.

Schliemann had encouraged his men to dig right through the real remains of Troy, destroying much of it in the process. The treasure, far from belonging to King Priam, dates from hundreds of years before the Trojan War.

During his life, historians mocked Schliemann for his amateurism. But his sheer determination and the strength of his belief did lead him to uncover secrets of a magnificent past ~ even if it wasn't the past he thought.

THE ILIAD: FACT OR FANTASY?

For a long time it was assumed that Homer's tales were totally mythical. But archaeological finds now suggest they may have had a basis in fact.

When Homer was writing, in 800BC, soldiers used small, round shields. Yet the warriors in his story of Troy, set several centuries before, fought with tall, curved ones. Pictures of tall shields, dating from long before Homer, have now been found in Greece.

Homer also said the walls of Troy were built by the gods, except for one inferior section that was built by men. The excavated walls do indeed have one badly

built area. How had Homer known what the city's walls were like?

The probable explanation is that stories about this period were passed down by word of mouth. Some parts inevitably changed in the telling, but other details, such as the shape of the shields, survived.

This vase from Mycenae was made in around 1200BC. Its decoration shows what soldiers wore at that time.

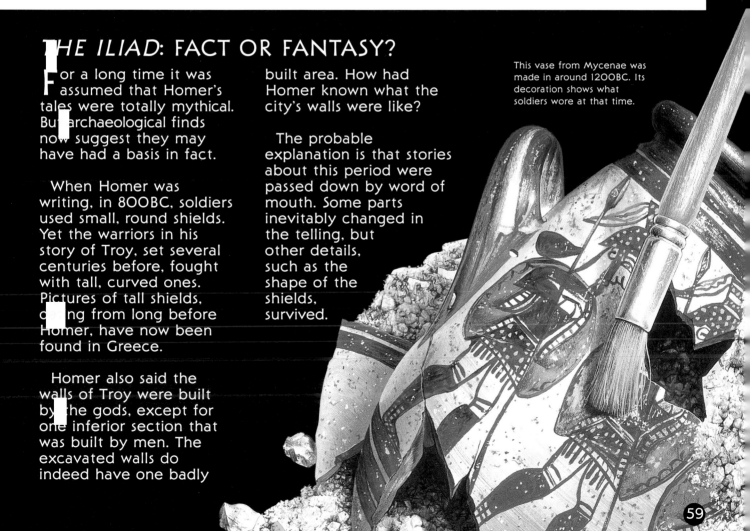

LOOT AND PLUNDER

Some ancient treasure isn't left to be retrieved by archaeologists. The Spanish conquistadors stole nearly all of the treasures of two ancient kingdoms in South America.

One of the biggest treasure hunts in history began in the years that followed the discovery of the New World (the American continent) in 1492. The treasure belonged to the Aztec and Inca empires in what are now Mexico and Peru, and was taken by the Spanish *conquistadors*, or conquerors, who explored and colonized these lands after they were discovered.

RICHES FOR THE TAKING

When gold and silver mines were found in the newly discovered lands, along with rich cities full of precious objects, many Europeans set out in the hope of making their fortune. Spain was the most active nation of all. It sent *conquistadors* to take over new land, convert the people to Christianity, and collect riches to send home.

This map of Central and South America shows today's borders.

One *conquistador*, Hernan Cortes, had already been living in Spanish-held Cuba when he decided to explore the Yucatan area, in what is now Mexico.

When he arrived with his army, the local people told him about their rulers, the Aztecs. Cortes decided to march to the Aztec capital, Tenochtitlan, to investigate.

Unluckily for the Aztecs, they believed in a pale-skinned and bearded god

called Quetzalcoatl. They assumed Cortes was this god, and their king, Montezuma, welcomed him with gifts of solid gold.

In return, Cortes and his men looted the city, captured Montezuma and eventually killed him. Tenochtitlan was destroyed. Much of the Aztec treasure was sent back to Spain to be melted down.

BARBARIANS

Cortes's actions now seem very cruel. As well as being greedy for money, he saw the Aztecs as primitive savages who deserved no respect. Their religion involved human sacrifice, and to European eyes this was barbaric ~ although the Atzecs also had a sophisticated society, with complex social structures and highly developed artistic skills.

An Aztec warrior with his spear and decorated shield.

OLD MEETS NEW

The *conquistadors* did not take everything. This little golden god was found recently in an ancient tomb in Peru.

Hernan Cortes

The discovery of the Americas was one of the most influential events in history. Neither the "Old World" nor the newly-discovered lands would ever be the same again. As well as hugely increasing the wealth of their own countries by looting New World gold and silver, *conquistadors* such as Hernan Cortes brought back crops previously unknown in Europe, such as potatoes, corn and tobacco. Meanwhile, many natives of the New World were converted to Christianity, and many more died from common European diseases like measles and chickenpox, which they had never encountered before.

The looting of the New World didn't stop with the Aztecs. Wave after wave of *conquistadors* arrived, hoping to claim some of the riches for themselves.

PIZARRO

One of these was Francisco Pizarro. An experienced Spanish explorer, he discovered the Inca empire during expeditions down the west coast of South America and asked for the Spanish king's consent to conquer the land he had found.

In 1532, Pizarro landed with an army in what is now Peru, and found a kingdom teeming with treasure. The temples were full of solid gold statues and ornaments, made by the Inca people to worship their sun god.

INCAS IN TROUBLE

When the Inca emperor, Atahualpa, came to greet his visitors, Pizarro didn't waste any time. He ordered his soldiers to open fire. The Incas only had wood and stone weapons which were no match for guns. Many of Atahualpa's men were killed, and he was imprisoned.

GOLD SPREE

The Spanish invaders then went about looting the country for treasure to send back to Spain. King Atahualpa soon realized the Spaniards wanted the gold for its own sake, rather than seeing the treasures as works of art. So he offered to fill a room once with gold, and twice with silver, to buy his freedom.

A BROKEN PROMISE

Pizarro agreed, and treasure was collected from all over the Inca kingdom. But when Atahualpa had carried out his promise, Pizarro killed him anyway and took over the kingdom, which became Peru.

Part of a 1.2m (4ft) high feather headdress, said to have belonged to King Montezuma of the Aztecs.

SECRETS OF THE STEPPES

*The Scythians were both terrifying warriors and sophisticated craftspeople,
but their civilization was almost unknown until their burial mounds were excavated.*

Many of the treasures discovered at burial sites across Asia have become precious museum pieces. But besides their innate value, they have given historians valuable clues about people and periods of the past.

TREASURE MOUNDS

The lands to the north of the Black Sea are dotted with thousands of strange mounds, known as kurgans. They are the burial mounds of a once-powerful people, the Scythians, who were famous for being fearless warriors.

A Greek historian called Herodotus (c. 480-425BC), wrote about their gruesome rituals, claiming they made drinking cups out of the skulls of their enemies. But he also described the Scythians as wealthy

and civilized, with great artistic traditions. Many later historians considered that Herodotus made up these tales, and few believed what he had said about the Scythians.

SURPRISE GIFT

In 1715, Peter the Great received a gift of some amazingly beautiful gold ornaments. But when he heard that they had been taken from a kurgan ~ a Scythian grave ~ he was shocked, and ordered that the

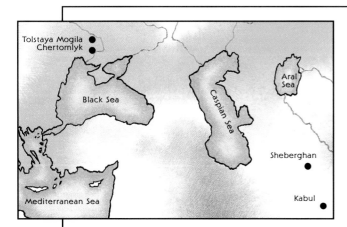

Scythian horsemen

looting must stop. Despite this, Scythian treasures continued to turn up from time to time.

In 1862, almost 150 years after Peter's order, the Russian government sent an archaeologist, I. E. Zabelin, to investigate a huge kurgan which was at Chertomlyk, on the Dnieper river. The government was eager to know what might be inside.

TREASURES IN THE TOMB

Zabelin decided to dig a trench across the middle of the kurgan, in order to reveal its inner structure. By the time workmen had dug the trench to a depth of 6m (20ft), they had unearthed over 250 horses' bridles. Many of these were covered in intricate decorations and studded with gold.

At the height of Scythian power, in the 4th century BC, Scythia covered most of modern-day Ukraine and the plains of southern Russia.

WHO WERE THE SCYTHIANS?

The Scythians were one of a group of tribes who inhabited the wide plains known as the Steppes, stretching eastwards from Hungary right across to the mountains of Kazakhstan. They were livestock farmers who kept herds of cattle and sheep. They were nomadic, and lived in wagons covered with protective tents which could be moved from place to place. In battles, which they had frequently, they fought on horseback, and were very successful warriors.

Deeper inside the kurgan was a carefully constructed grave, concealing a glittering hoard of treasure. There were two burial chambers. In the first lay two skeletons, both dressed in gold necklaces, bracelets and rings. In the second was a skeleton surrounded by precious ornaments made of silver, gold and electrum, which is a mixture of silver and gold.

Nearby lay another skeleton, which seemed to belong to a servant. She had probably been chosen to accompany her dead mistress on her journey to the next life.

This find prompted the Russians to excavate more kurgans. Some had already been looted by grave robbers, but many beautiful jewels and finely crafted ornaments were recovered, and preserved in the nation's museums.

GRAVE ROBBERS

The richest Scythian burial of all was found in 1971 by an archaeologist called Yevgeny Chernenko. At first, he thought the kurgan he was excavating, near Chertomlyk, had

been looted, as a tunnel had been dug through it.

A QUEEN AT REST

Then, as he fished in the mud, Chernenko felt a heavy golden object. It was a richly decorated gold pectoral (see below). Nearby was a secret burial chamber, one that the robbers had missed. It contained the skeleton of a Scythian queen.

She was wearing gold bangles and surrounded by the gold plaques that had decorated her robe; and her skull was covered by a solid gold headdress.

This gold neck ornament, or pectoral, was found near Chertomlyk, in the kurgan (burial mound) of a Scythian queen. It is intricately decorated with scenes from Scythian life and mythology.

63

THE PAINTINGS OF LASCAUX

An underground gallery of cave paintings, discovered by a group of teenagers, was almost destroyed by tourism before being rescued and preserved for future generations.

A cave system full of 20,000-year-old paintings was discovered on September 12, 1940 at Lascaux, near Montignac in France. It happened when Jacques Marsal's dog, Robot, got lost down a hole in the ground.

Jacques, a teenager at the time, was out with three friends, who agreed to wait while he climbed down into the hole in search of his pet. Suddenly, on the spot where Robot had vanished, the ground subsided.

Jacques was caught in an avalanche of falling earth and stones. When he picked himself up, he saw that he had found a cave. Immediately, he shouted to his friends.

Eager to explore the cave, the boys slid down into the hole, and set fire to a rag to give them some light. They were amazed to see that the walls and roof of the cave were daubed with white chalk, covered with bright images of animals ~ bulls, stags and cows ~ which resembled the prehistoric creatures they had seen in school textbooks.

The Lascaux cave paintings show a variety of animals such as bulls, stags and cows ~ probably beasts hunted by the people who depicted them.

Some of the images were small and delicate, but others were as long as a car. The boys suspected that they had stumbled upon something extraordinary and decided to return the next day armed with flashlights. This time, their investigations revealed two more caverns, both covered with similar paintings. Realizing the paintings must be important, they told their schoolteacher, Monsieur Laval. He told the local authorities of the discovery and soon a prehistoric expert, Abbé Henri Breuil, arrived to tour the caves and examine the pictures.

The pictures turned out to be over 200 centuries old, unique and priceless. They had probably been daubed onto the walls in near darkness, by artists using natural dyes.

Apart from their rarity value as art, the paintings could also tell historians something about the life of the prehistoric people who painted them ~ the only evidence left to subsequent generations.

TOURIST ATTRACTION

As word spread, the caves became a tourist site, though the escalation of World War Two meant the caves weren't flooded with

visitors. In 1948, however, when the caves were opened to the public, tourists came in their thousands. By 1962, over 1,500 people a day were visiting the paintings.

THE CAVES ARE CLOSED

But the atmosphere of the caves was altered by the arrival of so many visitors and the pictures began to fade. The French government had to act fast. In 1963, the caves were closed to the public, remaining open only to scientists for research purposes. One man stayed on though, as chief caretaker of the caves ~ Jacques Marsal, the man who had discovered them.

In the light of a burning rag, the boys were probably the first people in thousands of years to see the Lascaux paintings.

VISITOR DAMAGE

The very presence of hordes of tourists, in caves which had been deserted for thousands of years, was what caused the irreversible damage to the Lascaux paintings. The dampness from the breath of all the visitors accumulated in the caves, changing the atmosphere and causing green algae to grow on the walls. This damaged

the ancient pigments in the paintings, making them run and fade.

Many old works of art have to be protected from the effects of the human beings who come to look at them. Light, moisture, temperature changes and air movements can all damage ancient and delicate materials. This is why museum and gallery exhibits are sometimes displayed in a dim light, and are often kept behind glass, where the temperature and humidity (dampness) can be controlled.

ART TREASURE?

Is art really treasure? If it's the world's most famous painting ~ and it's been stolen ~ it is!

Probably the most famous painting on Earth, the *Mona Lisa* is a priceless treasure. When it went missing from its home in the Louvre gallery, Paris, in 1911, the world was shocked ~ especially as it did not seem to have been very carefully guarded at all.

The painting had been in France since its painter, Leonardo da Vinci, had brought it with him to Paris from Italy in the 1500s. It had been sold to the French king Francis I, and was eventually given to the Louvre in 1804.

THE LADY VANISHES

August 21, 1911 was a Monday, which meant the Louvre was closed all day for cleaning and repairs. A group of workmen admired the gallery's prize work of art, the portrait of Mona Lisa Gioconda, as they passed through the Salon Carré, the room where it hung, at 7:30 that morning. An hour later, however, when the workmen returned, the *Mona Lisa* was gone.

At first, the museum workers didn't worry. The *Mona Lisa* was often taken away to be photographed. When the painting had not reappeared by noon the next day, however, museum officials ordered a search. That afternoon, guards hunting through the gallery's basements and corridors, realized the painting really had been stolen when they found its familiar gilt frame propped against a wall in a storeroom. The frame was empty: the canvas itself had been carefully lifted out.

Above: the *Mona Lisa* ~ sometimes known as *La Gioconda* ~ by Leonardo da Vinci is probably the world's best-known artwork. The woman in the picture is famous for her enigmatic, mysterious smile.

The story of the theft soon reached the press, and when the evening newspapers came out Paris was thrown into shock at the terrible news.

IT'S A HOAX!

Many people refused to believe it, saying it must be a trick. Others thought perhaps it had been taken by an art student who was in love with the *Mona Lisa*'s enigmatic face, or by a thief who would demand an enormous ransom.

Two magazines offered large rewards for the painting's return. Meanwhile, at the Louvre, officials were fired and security was tightened after the embarrassing failure to guard an international treasure.

STRANGE LETTER

Despite all the gossip, there was no news of the *Mona Lisa* for over two years. Then, in November 1913, an Italian art dealer named Alfredo Geri received a mysterious letter. Its writer, who called himself "Leonard", said he had the *Mona Lisa*.

At first Geri thought the letter was a joke; but the next day he took it to Giovanni Poggi, director of the Uffizi Gallery in Florence, to see what he made of it. The two men decided to reply to Leonard, asking him to show them the painting. Within a week, they were invited to a hotel in Florence. A young man greeted Geri and Poggi and showed them into a dimly-lit room. Before going any further, though, he asked them for a sum of money in exchange for the *Mona Lisa*. The price he named was a tiny fraction of its real value.

UNDER THE BED

Then the man pulled out a trunk from under the bed. Inside, underneath an assortment of objects including a squashed hat and some tools, lay the painting. Soon Geri, Poggi and "Leonard", who turned out to be an Italian named Vincenzo Perugia, were at the Uffizi Gallery, where the painting's identity was verified and Perugia was arrested.

He said he'd stolen the painting in revenge for art treasures stolen from Italy in the 18th century, by the French emperor Napoleon Bonaparte. It had been easy, he said: he had simply walked into the Louvre, posed as a workman, and carried the *Mona Lisa* away.

After its rediscovery, the *Mona Lisa* was taken on a tour of Italy before being returned to Paris. Thousands of people turned out to see the painting they thought they had lost forever.

NATIONAL HERO

Perugia was sent to prison, but was released after a relatively short time of just seven months. Many Italians saw him as a hero for returning the *Mona Lisa* to her original homeland.

Leonardo's masterpiece, however, was soon back in the Salon Carré in the Louvre ~ and guarded far more carefully than it had been in 1911.

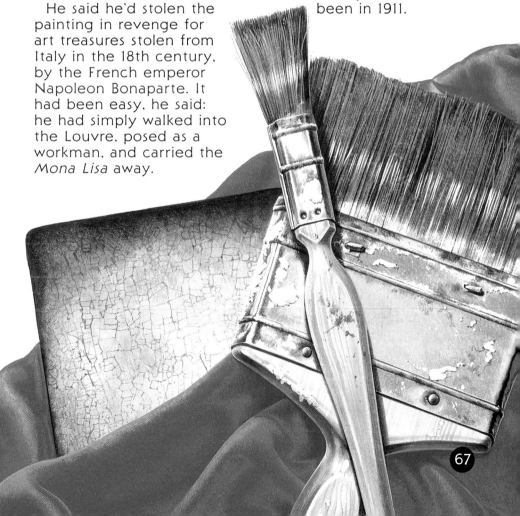

THE STORIES CONTINUE . . .

THREE LUCKY STRIKES (PAGE 7)

You can see the Mildenhall and Hoxne treasures on display at the British Museum in London, England. The treasure found at Snettisham after 1990, including the important collection of torques or neck rings, is also in the British Museum. The objects found at Snettisham before 1990, which include coins, torques and jewels, are exhibited at the Castle Museum in Norwich, near Snettisham.

A gold bracelet from the Hoxne treasure.

COCOS ISLAND (PAGE 10)

Although many treasure hunters think there is still treasure waiting to be found somewhere on Cocos Island, they can no longer try to find it. The island has been closed to all explorers and treasure hunters by the Costa Rican government.

GOLD FEVER (PAGE 12)

Treasure hunters still visit Superstition Mountain in Arizona, hoping to find the lost gold mine that made Don Miguel Peralta and Jacob Walz their fortunes. Several of those searching for the mine have met with violent ends, and the mine has yet to be rediscovered.

If this carved letter could ever be found, it might still lead to the Cocos Island treasure.

THE MONEY PIT (PAGE 14)

The Money Pit has not been reopened since it collapsed and flooded; although Triton Alliance, one of the companies involved in the search for treasure there, still carries out excavations on the site.

TREASURE ISLANDS (PAGE 22)

In 1997, a sunken ship, which may be Blackbeard's flagship, the *Queen Anne's Revenge*, was found off the coast of North Carolina. If it is Blackbeard's, it will be only the second pirate ship ever to be found. The first is the *Whydah* (see page 37).

Gold nuggets in their natural state.

THE SPOILS OF WAR (PAGE 18)

After World War Two ended in 1945, the Allies (the group of countries which had made up the winning side in the war) set up an organization called the Tripartite Gold Commission. Its aim was to return all the currency and gold treasures stolen by the Nazis to their countries of origin.

But the Commission found it impossible to agree on how much the Nazis had stolen and where it had gone. Much of it had been deposited in bank accounts in Switzerland, which had been a neutral country throughout the war. In 1946, the Swiss repaid £40 million ($65 million), worth about £440 million ($700 million) today; but refused to pay out any more, despite the fact that several substantial claims remained unpaid.

In September 1996, news broke that about £40 million ($65 million) more than had previously been reported was still stored in Swiss banks. A conference was held in London in 1997, to decide how to distribute the gold. About 40 countries attended, but the matter wasn't completely decided. The debate continues.

GHOST GALLEONS
(PAGE 25)

Mel Fisher, the treasure hunter who found the "Ghost Galleons", believes that the thousands of emeralds his team found on the seabed around the wreck of the *Atocha* had been smuggled aboard illegally, as they do not appear on the ship's official cargo list. Most of the treasure from the wreck is now held by two museums in Florida, although some items are in other museums around the world.

Mel Fisher still works in the treasure industry, coordinating treasure hunts and developing and improving treasure-hunting equipment.

THE VASA COMES HOME
(PAGE 28)

Archaeologists spent five months picking 14,000 objects out of the thick, black mud inside the *Vasa*'s hull after the wreck had been towed back into Stockholm. Then, over a period of 17 years, the wreck was sprayed with a solution of preservative chemicals. Finally, it was very slowly dried out and some repairs were made. The *Vasa* went on display at last in June 1990, as the main exhibit in a new museum in Stockholm.

AN ICY GRAVE (PAGE 32)

As a direct result of the tragic loss of the *Titanic*, ships are now required by law to carry enough lifeboats to evacuate all aboard.

Experts estimate that within a century the *Titanic*'s iron hull will have rusted away. In the meantime, there is much debate about what to do with the wreck. Robert Ballard, along with many of the relatives of those who died, wanted it to be left alone. They did not want anyone to profit from selling or displaying *Titanic* artefacts.

More items have been recovered, however, and there are plans to build a floating museum to tour and display them. The National Maritime Museum in London and the company RMS Titanic have set up a committee to try to protect the wreck site from thieves.

A QUEST FOR PIRATE PLUNDER (PAGE 37)

Barry Clifford, who found the wreck of the *Whydah*, has not sold any of the treasures from the pirate ship. Instead, many of them are displayed in his own museum in Provincetown, Massachusetts, USA. There, visitors can see restoration work in progress; and some of the objects from the wreck have formed a touring exhibition.

This pirate pistol, found on the *Whydah*, is now on display to the public.

Clifford believes that so far he has only recovered around 20% of the treasure that the *Whydah* was carrying. He is working on a project to raise and recover the rest of the sunken cargo.

69

CHINA CARGO
(PAGE 40)

After the sale of the Nanking china found on the *Geldermalsen*, Michael Hatcher, the treasure hunter who discovered it, used some of the proceeds to buy a large cattle ranch in Australia. He still works on treasure hunts in the South China Sea.

ARCTIC EXPEDITION
(PAGE 42)

Keith Jessop, whose company Jessop Marine successfully recovered the *HMS Edinburgh*'s gold cargo, now lives in France and is still involved in undersea treasure salvage work.

The wreck stayed on the seabed, but the *HMS Belfast*, the *Edinburgh*'s sister ship, is now a floating museum on the River Thames in London, England. It is very similar to the *Edinburgh*, and visitors can go on board and explore it.

THE PHARAOH'S TOMB
(PAGE 47)

Four years after the mummified body of Tutankhamun was first unwrapped, Howard Carter supervised the pharaoh's reburial. The body was wrapped in linen, placed in the outer stone sarcophagus, or coffin, it had been found in, and returned to the burial chamber, where it remains today. The rest of the tomb's treasures are now in Cairo Museum in Egypt.

Howard Carter himself spent the last years of his life writing and lecturing about the famous tomb he had discovered. When he died on March 2, 1939, very little fuss was made by the newspapers, despite their earlier claims of a curse.

An injury found on the back of the pharaoh's skull sparked a renewed argument among historians about how Tutankhamun had died. It is still being debated.

Tutankhamun's mummy is on display in its stone coffin in the original tomb, but the outer coffins can be seen in the Cairo Museum.

AN UNDERGROUND ARMY
(PAGE 53)

A painted terracotta warrior from Huang Di's tomb.

The first pit at Huang Di's tomb, found in 1974, held 6,000 clay soldiers. Subsequently another three pits were unearthed. Pit 2 (found in 1976) contains archers, footsoldiers and chariots. Pit 3 (1977) holds more soldiers, and Pit 4 (1977) appears never to have been filled. A full excavation of Pit 2 is currently underway, and in 1994 a museum was built over the top of the pit to allow visitors to watch the archaeologists at work. Around two million people a year visit it. Huang Di's burial chamber itself will only be opened when the other artefacts have been dealt with.

IN SEARCH OF LEGENDS (PAGE 56)

Heinrich Schliemann left the Trojan treasures he'd found to his homeland, Germany, but they vanished after World War Two. They turned up in 1996 in Moscow, where Russian troops had taken them in 1945. The treasures went on display in Moscow, but both Germany and Turkey claim to have rights to them.

One of the treasures Schliemann gave to Germany.

LOOT AND PLUNDER (PAGE 60)

Much of the treasure from Spain's South American colonies was taken back to Europe and melted down, destroying forever the unique designs and details of the objects.

But some South American treasure did survive. A group of Incas are thought to have escaped to the city of Machu Picchu, high up in the Andes mountains. After a failed revolt against the Spaniards in 1536, the city fell into ruins. It was rediscovered in 1911, and is now a major tourist site. Visitors can still see original Inca architecture and craftsmanship there.

The lost Inca city of Machu Picchu.

THE PAINTINGS OF LASCAUX (PAGE 64)

One of the Lascaux paintings, showing a large animal.

The Lascaux caves were closed to the public in the early 1960s, so that experts could work on protecting and preserving the damaged paintings. Twenty years later, in 1982, a replica of two of the main caves in the system was opened to tourists. It contains replica paintings created using the same techniques, tools and materials as the prehistoric artists used, and is known as Lascaux II. Jacques Marsal, who discovered the original caves, continues to work as a guide there.

ART TREASURE? (PAGE 66)

In January 1915, after serving seven months of his jail sentence for stealing the *Mona Lisa*, Vincenzo Perugia was released because of ill health. He eventually returned to his home town of Dumenza, Italy, in 1921, and married a cousin. He took his wife back to southeastern France, and the couple ran a paint store there until Perugia died in 1947.

A portrait of *Mona Lisa*'s artist, Leonardo da Vinci.

The Hotel Tripoli-Italia in Paris, where Perugia had lived with the *Mona Lisa* stashed in his trunk, was renamed Hotel La Gioconda after the woman in the famous painting.

GLOSSARY

airlift A device for sucking mud away from a submerged shipwreck.

Apaches A tribe of native Americans who once inhabited the area now covered by New Mexico and Arizona.

archaeologist A scientist who studies the remains and ruins of old civilizations.

Aztecs The native people who inhabited most of what is now Mexico, before the area was conquered by Spain in the 16th century.

bends, the An illness caused by gas bubbles forming in the blood due to changes in pressure, often suffered by deep-sea divers.

boatswain An officer on a ship, responsible for organizing the crew and equipment.

bow The front end of a boat or ship.

canopic jars Jars used by the Ancient Egyptians for preserving dead body parts.

Celts A group of tribes who inhabited parts of Western Europe from about 1,000BC.

Cold War A period of non-violent hostility during the years after World War Two between Russia and the western powers, including the USA and Britain.

concretions Hard, crusty mineral deposits which form on objects under the sea.

conquistadors Spanish conquerors who took over parts of Central and South America in the 16th and 17th centuries.

core sampler A device which cuts cork-sized chunks out of buried or sunken objects, and brings them up to be analyzed.

death mask A mask, usually made of precious metals, placed over the face of a dead body before it is buried.

diving bell An air-filled, bell-shaped vessel in which divers can be lowered underwater.

diving engine A device with an air supply, which can be lowered underwater holding one diver.

doubloon A type of Spanish gold coin.

dry dock a narrow channel into which a boat or ship can be floated, before the water is pumped out to allow repairs to take place on the hull.

electrum An alloy, or mixture, of gold and silver.

embalm To preserve a dead body by removing the organs, drying it out and covering it with ointments.

excavate To uncover archaeological ruins or buried objects by digging carefully around them.

forty-niner A miner or gold prospector who joined the American Gold Rush of 1849.

galleon A large sailing ship with several decks and masts, usually used for trade or war.

galley or **gally** A narrow, single-decked sailing ship.

griffin A mythical creature, usually with the head and wings of an eagle and the body of a lion.

gunport A door in the side of a ship out of which a cannon can be fired.

hull The outer shell and framework of a boat or ship.

Incas A South American tribe who inhabited the area that is now Peru, before it was conquered by Spain in the 16th century.

ingot An oblong block or bar of metal, especially gold or silver.

jade A precious bluish-green mineral.

junk A flat-bottomed sailing boat used in eastern Asia.

kurgan A type of burial mound found in Siberia and central Asia.

lapis lazuli A bright blue semi-precious stone.

magnetometer A device for detecting large amounts of metal underwater.

metal detector A machine that uses magnetism to find metal objects underground.

Ming period The period when the Ming dynasty ruled China, from the 1400s to the 1700s, during which a large amount of highly decorated porcelain, known as Ming china, was produced.

moon-pool A hole in the bottom of a ship for divers to dive through.

mummy A dead body, especially in Ancient Egypt, which has been preserved by being embalmed, wrapped in cloth and buried.

natron A chemical salt found in Egypt, used by the Ancient Egyptians to dry and preserve dead bodies.

Nazis A shortened name for the German National Socialist Party, led by Hitler in the 1920s and 1930s when he was planning to conquer Europe.

New World North, Central and South America, which were seen as "new" by the Europeans who discovered them in the 15th century.

nomadic A word used to describe tribes or people who move from place to place as a way of life.

obsidian A deep blue or black stone with a glassy texture.

oceanographer A scientist who studies oceans and seas.

pectoral A jewel or ornament designed to be worn on the chest.

piece of eight A Spanish dollar or gold coin.

pirate A sea bandit; someone who attacks ships at sea and steals their cargo, or takes over and steals the ships themselves.

propwash A device for blasting water at the seabed to clear mud away from shipwrecks.

reef A ridge or platform of rock, sand or coral, lying just under the surface of the sea.

Romans The people of Ancient Rome, who extended their empire to cover most of Europe and parts of Africa and Asia.

salvage To rescue or retrieve something, especially sunken treasure.

sarcophagus A stone coffin.

Saxons A tribe originally from Northern Europe, who conquered parts of southern and eastern Britain.

scatter A trail of treasure and debris on the seabed which may lead to a shipwreck.

Scythians Ancient tribes, famous for their fearlessness in war, who lived in the area north of the Black Sea, in what is now Russia and Ukraine.

seal An imprint made in wet clay, wax or another soft substance, as a mark of a particular person or thing.

shipworm A type of sea mollusc with a very long, thin body, which eats through underwater wood, and can damage shipwrecks.

sonar scanner A device which detects underwater objects by sending out sound signals, and then collecting and analyzing the echoes they make when they bounce against things.

submersible A type of mini-submarine, which may be remotely operated from the surface, or may carry a small number of people.

terracotta A kind of red clay.

torque A neck ring used either as a decoration or as protection in battle.

U-boat A German submarine (taken from the German word *Unterseeboot*, which means undersea boat).

vomit pot A bowl designed for being sick in during a heavy meal.

yu-xia Ancient Chinese burial suits made of jade.

WHO'S WHO

This who's who is an at-a-glance guide to the treasure hunters, pirates, explorers, archaeologists and buried monarchs and aristocrats whose stories are told in this book.

Akhenaten Pharaoh (Ancient Egyptian king) who ruled before Tutankhamun.

Atahualpa King of the Incas when they were conquered by Francisco Pizarro.

Ballard, Robert Scientist who discovered the wreck of the *Titanic*.

Bellamy, "Black Sam" Pirate who drowned when the *Whydah* pirate ship sank.

Bergmans, Petrus Castaway who claimed he had found treasure on Cocos Island.

Blackbeard (Edward Teach) Famous and much-feared pirate who scared his victims by wearing burning fuses in his beard.

Blankenship, Dan Treasure hunter who investigated the Money Pit.

Bonito, Benito Portuguese pirate who hid his stolen treasure on Cocos Island.

Breuil, Abbé Henri Expert on prehistory who investigated the Lascaux cave paintings.

Burton, Captain Francis British army officer who discovered the Oxus treasure.

Butcher, Gordon Farmworker who found the Mildenhall Roman treasure in a field.

Carnarvon, Lord Aristocrat who funded the search for Tutankhamun's tomb.

Carter, Howard Archaeologist who found and excavated Tutankhamun's tomb.

Chernenko, Yevgeny Archaeologist who found a Scythian queen's grave in a kurgan (burial mound).

Clifford, Barry Treasure hunter who found the wreck of the *Whydah* pirate ship.

Cortes, Hernan Spanish conqueror who invaded the land of the Aztecs and took many of their treasures.

Da, Marchioness of Ancient Chinese aristocrat whose body was preserved in a treasure-filled tomb.

Dagobert II A seventh-century king of France.

Davies, Edward A pirate who used Cocos Island as a base for his raids.

Denarnaud, Marie Housekeeper of the mysteriously wealthy priest Berenger Saunière who knew the whereabouts of his secret treasure supply.

Dou Wan Wife of Ancient Chinese Prince Lui Sheng, who, like him, was buried in a suit of jade pieces.

Elizabeth I English queen who sent her navy to defeat the Spanish Armada in 1588.

Falting, Per Edvin Diver who was the first to find the wreck of the *Vasa* warship.

Fisher, Mel Treasure hunter who found the wrecks of the treasure ships *Atocha* and *Margarita* (the "Ghost Galleons").

Ford, Sidney Farmer who kept the Mildenhall treasure for several years after it was found on his land.

Foss, Colonel Treasure hunter who searched for treasure on the Tobermory Galleon, with no success.

Franzen, Anders Swedish engineer who helped to raise the *Vasa*.

Geri, Alfredo Italian art dealer who rediscovered the *Mona Lisa*.

Gissler, August Treasure hunter who was left Benito Bonito's treasure map, but failed to find riches on Cocos Island.

Grimm, Jack Oil tycoon who hoped to find the wreck of the *Titanic*, but failed.

Gustav II King of Sweden who had the *Vasa* warship built in 1628.

Gustav Adolf VI King of Sweden who presided over the raising of the *Vasa*.

Hatcher, Michael Treasure hunter who found the wreck of the *Geldermalsen* and its cargo of tea and china.

Henry VIII King of England who had the *Mary Rose* warship refurbished in 1545.

Herodotus Ancient Greek historian who wrote about the Scythians.

Hitler, Adolf German leader who planned to take over Europe in the 1930s.

Homer Ancient Greek poet who wrote *The Iliad*, telling the story of the city of Troy.

Huang Di The first emperor of China, whose tomb was guarded by an army of terracotta (clay) soldiers.

Jessop, Keith Treasure hunter who retrieved gold from the wreck of the *HMS Edinburgh* warship.

Keating, John Treasure hunter who found the

pirate William Thompson's treasure on Cocos Island.

Kidd, Captain William Sea captain turned pirate who hid his stolen treasure on Gardiner's Island.

Lafitte, Jean and Pierre Pirate brothers who were based on Galveston Island, where treasure is still thought to be buried.

Lawes, Eric Amateur treasure hunter who found the Hoxne Roman treasure while using a metal detector to look for a lost hammer.

Leonardo da Vinci Famous Italian artist and scientist, who painted the *Mona Lisa* in about 1506.

Lister, Moira Actress who tried unsuccessfully to find treasure on Cocos Island.

Lui Sheng Ancient Chinese prince who was buried in a suit of Jade, which was meant to preserve his body.

Lupicinus Roman general whose name was inscribed on the Mildenhall treasure.

Lyon, Eugene Historian who helped Mel Fisher find the "Ghost Galleons".

Maclean Scottish chieftain who befriended the sailors on the Tobermory Galleon, before it blew up and sank.

Marchioness of Da *see* Da, Marchioness of.

Marsal, Jacques French teenager who discovered the Lascaux caves and later became a guide there.

McGinnis, Daniel Treasure hunter who was the first to dig, unsuccessfully, for treasure at the Money Pit.

McKee, Alexander Journalist who worked to find and raise the wreck of the *Mary Rose* warship.

Montezuma King of the Aztecs when they were invaded and conquered by

Hernan Cortes.

Napoleon French emperor who stole art treasures from Italy during the 18th century.

Peralta, Don Miguel Treasure hunter who revealed the location of a secret gold mine in Arizona to Jacob Walz.

Perugia, Vincenzo Thief who stole the *Mona Lisa* from the Louvre gallery in Paris, and took it to Italy.

Peter the Great 18th-century czar (leader) of Russia, who received gifts of treasure stolen from a kurgan (burial mound).

Philip II Spanish king who sent the Spanish Armada to attack England in 1588.

Pizarro, Francisco Spanish explorer who conquered the Inca empire in the early 1500s.

Plouviez, Judith Archaeologist who investigated the Hoxne treasure, and secretly took it to the British Museum.

Poggi, Giovanni Director of the Uffizi art gallery, who was invited to help retrieve the stolen *Mona Lisa*.

Quetzalcoatl Pale-skinned, bearded god of the Aztecs. They thought the conqueror Cortes was Quetzalcoatl when he arrived.

Restall, Bob Treasure hunter who died after mysteriously falling down the Money Pit.

Rossier, John Deep-sea diver who was the first to find gold on the wreck of the *HMS Edinburgh*.

Rowe, Jacob Inventor who designed a diving engine to look for treasure on the Tobermory Galleon.

Rule, Margaret Archaeologist who raised

the *Mary Rose* warship.

Saunière, Berenger French priest who became rich after finding some strange coded documents.

Schliemann, Heinrich Amateur treasure hunter who uncovered important ruins at Troy and Mycenae.

Southack, Captain Investigator sent to retrieve the *Whydah*'s treasure after it sank.

Stamatkis Archaeologist who helped Heinrich Schliemann find treasure-filled tombs at Mycenae.

Stephen, Saint 11th-century Hungarian king whose crown was among treasure stolen by the Nazis.

Tantum, Bill Expert who helped Robert Ballard find the wreck of the *Titanic*.

Teach, Edward *see* Blackbeard.

Thompson, William Sailor who was entrusted with taking treasure from Peru to Panama. He stole it and hid it on Cocos Island.

Tutankhamun Pharaoh (Ancient Egyptian king) who was buried in an opulent tomb after dying (possibly by being murdered) at 19.

da Vinci, Leonardo *see* Leonardo da Vinci.

Walz, Jacob German miner who went to Arizona and found out about a hidden gold mine. He became rich and murdered anyone who discovered his secret.

Weiser, Jacob Prospector who helped Jacob Walz, but was killed by Apaches.

Whatling, Peter Farmer on whose land the Hoxne treasure was found.

Zabelin, I. E. Archaeologist who first investigated Scythian kurgans (burial mounds) in Russia.

International Treasure Map

This treasure map of the world shows all the treasure sites described in this book. The different kinds of treasure are shown by different symbols.

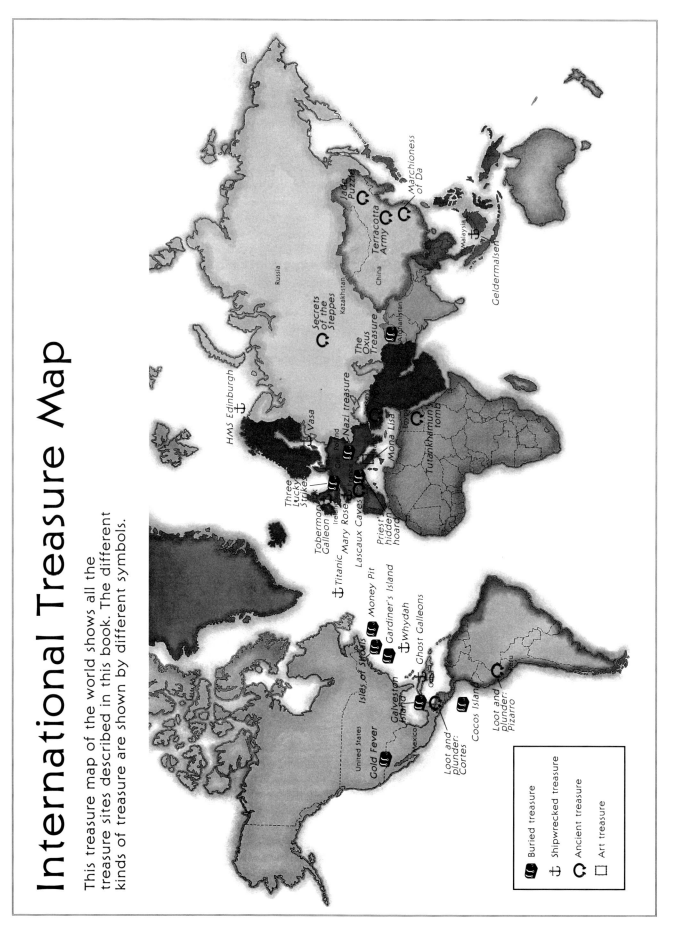

INDEX

The publishers are grateful to the following organizations and individuals for their kind permission to reproduce material:

p6: Tutankhamun statue, Robert Harding Picture Library;
p11: Moira Lister, Popperfoto;
p12 and p13: gold prospectors, Corbis-Bettman;
p14: Bob Restall and family, Herald Photo;
p16: Captain Francis Burton, The British Museum
p17: armlet artwork based on a photograph of the Oxus treasure, © The British Museum;
p18: treasure in Kaiseroda Mine, National Archives, Still Picture Branch;
p21: Berenger Saunière, l'abbé saunière;
p25: Diver checking seabed, Pat Clyne;
p26: Diver with emeralds, Pat Clyne;
p28: the *Vasa*'s maiden voyage, Bjorn Landström;
p28: carved beam from the *Vasa*, Vasa Museum, Sweden;
p28: the *Vasa* in dry dock, Vasa Museum, Sweden;
p30: the *Mary Rose*, Pepys Library, Magdalene College, Cambridge;
p30: text taken from a painting of the *Mary Rose*, Pepys Library, Magdalene College, Cambridge;
p31: hull of the *Mary Rose*, The Mary Rose Trust;
p32 and p69: the *Titanic* in Belfast Lough, Ulster Folk & Transport Museum (H1721/CO74);
p34: *Argo* on seabed artwork based on an illustration by Ken Marshall, ©1987, from *The Discovery of the Titanic*, a Warner/Madison Press book;
p34: *Argo* diagram artwork based on an illustration by Jack McMaster, ©1990, from *The Discovery of the Bismarck*, a Hodder & Stoughton/Madison Press book;
p35: the *Titanic* on the seabed, Sygma/Titanic Archives (229640 30);
p36: Jacob Rowe's diving engine, National Maritime Museum, Greenwich, England (C5697/A);
p37: the *Whydah*'s last moments, artist: John Barkey, Whydah Joint Venture, Inc.;
p38: Barry Clifford, Maritime Explorations, Inc.;
p39: "Black Sam" Bellamy, artist: Ron Fowler, Whydah Joint Venture, Inc.;
p41: crate being raised from the *Geldermalsen*, Christie's, Amsterdam;
p43: *HMS Edinburgh* sinking, Barry Penrose;
p47: Howard Carter and Lord Carnarvon photo, HVF Winstone;
p52: jade funeral suit, Robert Harding Picture Library;
p53: terracotta warriors, Robert Harding Picture Library;
p57: Sophia Schliemann, Ancient Art & Architecture Ltd.;
p58: "Mask of Agamemnon", Ancient Art & Architecture Ltd.;
p64 and p71: Lascaux cave painting, AKG photo;
p66: the *Mona Lisa* by Leonardo da Vinci, Louvre, Paris, France/Bridgeman Art Library.

Every effort has been made to trace the copyright holders of material in this book. If any rights have been omitted, the publishers offer their apologies and will rectify this in any subsequent editions following notification.